Lord,
Please Meet Me
in the Laundry Room

Lord, Please Meet Me in the Laundry Room

Heavenly Help for Earthly Moms

Barbara Curtis

Beacon Hill Press of Kansas City
Kansas City, Missouri

Copyright 2004
By Barbara Curtis and Beacon Hill Press of Kansas City

ISBN 083-412-0976

Printed in the
United States of America

Library of Congress Cataloging-in-Publication Data

Curtis, Barbara, 1948-
   Lord, please meet me in the laundry room : heavenly help for earthly moms / Barbara Cur-
tis.
      p. cm.
Includes bibliographical references.
   ISBN 0-8341-2097-6 (pbk.)
   1. Mothers—Religious life. 2. Motherhood—Religious aspects—Christianity. I. Title.

   BV4529.18.C87 2004
   248.8'431—dc22

                                                            2003025797

10   9   8   7   6   5   4   3   2   1

To my husband and best friend, Tripp,
who was there to help God bring out the best in me.

Contents

Introduction

What drives a mother to pick up a book about mothering? I mean, it's not like we have a lot of time to read. If you're like me, then it might be the vague feeling that since we've got questions —how do we find more patience/organization/discipline/ happiness?—someone must have the answers.

And judging from the titles of parenting books, lots of authors think they do—conveniently distilled into seven steps or 50 ways. Some even claim to have the inside track on how God wants this parenting thing done.

Some books that promise to make life with children better actually end up making it worse. After reading them we feel burdened and guilty because the ideas are easier said than done. We're always measuring ourselves and so often falling short.

This book isn't about that at all. This book is about spending some time together sorting through the things that get in the way of finding joy in motherhood. It's about getting real about the past and mistakes we've made, the limitations of our lifestyle as mothers, the competitive spirit that robs us of intimacy with other mothers, and the lack of affirmation that sometimes makes us want to cry.

This is a book about seizing each day, squeezing every bit of joy from every peanut-butter-and-jelly-smeared moment, finding God in the hum of a washing machine or an unexpected bargain. It's about learning to believe that the stock market, the international situation, the Fortune 500 are really inconsequential next to the work we do—in God's eyes, at least. And that's what really counts.

Motherhood turns out to be where it's happening, after all.

God sees it all. He sees our daily struggles as mothers—physical, emotional, spiritual—and He waits for us to cast our cares upon Him. He says, "Come to me all you who are weary and burdened, and I will give you rest" (Matt. 11:28).

I believe this in my bones. I believe it because as a mother of 12, I live it each day and have for some time. But I believe it, too, because my life took some unusual and crazy twists and turns before I found the straight and narrow. And my relationship with God once I found Him—already well on my way to being a mega-mom—turned out to be as real and vital as the gravitational force that keeps me from spinning away into space.

This is really the story of the interplay between my motherhood and my faith, because I believe that without my children, I couldn't have learned the things I've learned. And without my faith, I'd have been too busy conforming to others' expectations to learn to be the mother God wanted me to be.

Every mother finding the time to read this—between laundry and lunches, diapers and dinners—is in the midst of her own spiritual journey. My dream—the dream that keeps me at my keyboard when I'd rather take a nap, the dream that wakes me up at night to write down things I need to say—is that you will find the hope and the glory in your motherhood that I found in mine.

May God bless and keep you—through all the trials and smiles of motherhood—and through them draw you nearer to Him each day!

Barbara Curtis
Waterford, Virginia
September 2003

❧ 1 ❧

The Chapel of the Wash and Dry

It can't be morning already.

Everything outside me is saying *yes, it is,* but everything within still says *no!* The alarm sounds like a faraway foghorn. My body feels weighed down with anchors and my eyelids are stuck at half-mast. I heave myself over to peek at the time. Six o'clock and already the day's not adding up: although I went to bed at 11:00, I feel like I've only gotten a few hours sleep.

With the shock of a shipwreck it hits me—I *have* only gotten a few hours sleep!

Awareness washes up in waves, bearing glimpses of scenes from the night before: Joshua coughing up a storm quelled only with cough syrup, Benjamin sobbing for a prayer to soothe away a bad dream, baby Jonathan calling for his lullaby tape, Zachary's wet bed.

And how could I forget being startled at 3 A.M. to find Sophia hovering silently at my bedside, waiting politely for her mommy to open her eyes? I guess she wanted quality time.

"Count it all joy," I mutter as I sit up and—not wanting to break my meager momentum—lunge for the laundry room.

The slick linoleum under my feet is a wake-up call. Once over the threshold, my body carries me through the familiar routine of stuffing sheets into the washer, measuring soap, and setting dials. The whoosh of the water into the machine is refreshing, like a splash of cool water on my face.

Contemplating the mounds of clothes around me, I am re-minded and reassured:

> I lift up my eyes to the hills—
> where does my help come from?
> My help comes from the LORD,
> the Maker of heaven and earth (Ps. 121:1-2).

Here is where I get a second wind. Here is where, like a ship-wrecked survivor, I grab the life preserver of the Lord. Because, Lord knows, He is the only One who can get me through this day.

≈≈≈≈≈≈

It wasn't always this way. I used to think my laundry room was just a laundry room. This is the story of how I learned how much more it could be—and how much more I could be—once I let it become more than just a place to wash my family's clothes.

I was a new Christian 16 years ago, and the world was a differ-ent and delightful place. I'd finally met God and knew He loved me. With 30-some years of ramshackle living behind me, I finally felt secure—and suddenly alive, like the sleeping princess awak-ened by the prince to find the perfect happy ending.

Really, it was just the beginning.

I'd been a believer for just a few weeks when I signed up for my first women's Bible study. It was there that I began to see my inadequacies on parade.

I hadn't grown up with the Bible and so was starting from scratch. That was bad enough. But worse, I suddenly found myself surrounded by a bunch of wonderful women with flawless hair and hands who made it look easy to look good. For me, it wasn't so easy. With seven children at home—six under 10—my morn-ing had been pretty hectic just trying to detach. All I had to do was tilt my head a little to the left for a pungent reminder of my motherhood—the smell of spit-up on the shoulder of the T-shirt I'd had no time to change before dashing out, only to arrive late as usual anyway.

I kept my hands folded to hide my scruffy, half-bitten finger-nails, but there was nothing I could do about the rose tattoo on my right hand—the most visible of three acquired during my 1960s and 1970s hippie days. In 1987 there just weren't many women sporting tattoos—especially in Bible studies.

Would they wonder if I was a real Christian? I mean, I had no doubts about my faith, but I worried that they would. After all, there was no way for me to stand up and announce, *"Oh, by the way, I got this tattoo a long time ago before I knew the Lord, before I understood the emptiness inside that drove me to fill it in ways that would never work. All I ever really wanted was to feel special. And now that I know God, I do. I'm just stuck with this tattoo to remind me what it was like without Him."*

Now I was sure I was special in God's eyes—well, maybe al-most sure. Little doubts were prowling like critters around my new spiritual shelter, looking for just the teensiest crack to slip through. And sometimes they'd find one.

Which is why sometimes in Bible study, I'd catch myself won-dering if some were more favored than others. I was so far be-hind! I was 39, just learning the difference between the Old and New Testament, scrambling to locate certain verses in my pain-fully obvious new-looking Bible.

Others seemed to find them with their eyes closed. Their Bibles had quilted covers that unzipped to reveal well-worn pages, notated here, there, and everywhere with things they'd been learn-ing during the years I'd wasted on things like rose tattoos. Things they'd learned in years of Bible studies and hours of *quiet time.*

Oh, the concept of quiet time! It loomed over my life with the gravitas of a Goodyear blimp, a constant reminder of yet an-other something I needed to do. Another something on the crowded list of things I woke up every morning with every inten-tion of accomplishing, then regretted not doing at the end of the day when life with my family left me too pooped to pop.

Another something to feel guilty about.

Long about the third week someone mentioned a *prayer closet*—as in "I fled to my prayer closet and poured my heart out to the Lord"—which I took to be a place where a believer could find solutions to the weightiest problems, a place that maybe if I had one I could make my quiet time come true.

Ah, so that must be what was missing! I needed a prayer closet to flee to. Unfortunately, when I hurried home to look for some previously uncharted territory to call my own, I could find nowhere with the sustained privacy necessary for even a prayer shoebox.

Not with the hordes in my house.

Maybe that was my problem—too many children. Lord knows, I'd been hearing that enough, as in "I don't know how you do it—two's all I can handle" or "I just don't have the patience" or worse, "I'd go crazy with that many kids."

Actually, I'd want to say, *two used to be all I could handle. I wasn't patient myself until I had a lot of kids*, and *How do you know you won't go crazy without them?*

Then, too, I kept hearing that God didn't give us more than we could handle. So He must expect me to handle it and measure up to all the Christian stuff I was supposed to do too.

Weeks went by as I pondered these things in my heart, battling my growing sense of self-doubt. In so many ways my life was getting better and better—more patience with my husband and children, more enthusiasm for my life at home. But in the spiritual arena, I wasn't making the progress I thought I should. I mean, not only could I not find a prayer closet or quiet time, some weeks I waited till the night before to answer a week's worth of questions in our Bible study book—even though our leader had warned us not to.

Some weeks I never got to them at all.

Day after day, I'd think I'd get a start on developing a spiritual life, and day after day I'd fail. My days were already way too crowded, but even when I'd carefully plan some quality time with God, something unexpected would set me back—from small things like runny noses and broken plates and stitches to major events. As when two-year-old busiest-boy-in-the-world Benjamin brought in a garden hose to water our green carpet—just like Daddy and the grass!—causing a tidal wave that left behind pulled-up soggy carpets and a week of roaring turbo fans.

"Honey, the hose is for outside only," I'd said calmly, removing the hose and walking it outside as though this wasn't one of the greatest domestic disasters I'd ever seen. It wouldn't help to get mad at my little boy. After all, Ben was driven by every toddler's desire to serve, the same one that moved him to shovel all the ashes from one fireplace and try to carry them to another. No way he could possibly understand what he did was wrong.

So, yes, I was calm. And any mother who's had to clean up the consequences of a child's innocent attempts at helping will know what I mean when I say how proud of myself I was for not losing it. Moments like that at least made me feel like I was on the path to becoming a good mother, though there was always plenty to keep me humble.

But would I ever become the believer I wanted to be? Evidently not with little people like Ben consuming every available minute in my life.

One day in the laundry room, while wrestling with the lights and darks, I wrestled with my dilemma. *Oh, Lord,* I thought, *is there a prayer closet somewhere for me? And what about this thing they call quiet time?*

Aren't you praying now? This question was wordlessly impressed upon my heart. It was a question, but it was an answer. And I hadn't expected an answer, so it caught me off guard. But I knew who it came from.

Yes, but, Lord . . . and things began to spill out of my heart that I hardly knew were there. They spilled out even as I was real-izing how much He already knew.

I didn't have to tell Him how hard it was to feel like a light-weight when others had more spiritual muscle to flex. He already knew.

I didn't have to tell Him how much I wanted to be the best I could be, and how far from the best I often felt. He already knew.

I didn't have to tell Him how much I missed the afterglow of the decision that changed my life forever, now clouded by my frustration with my inability to jump through the hoops I thought I should. He already knew.

I didn't have to tell Him that no matter what, I would follow Him. He already knew.

I didn't have to tell Him anything about me, because He al-ready knew everything there was to know.

But since I knew He was listening, I told Him anyway. And somehow He gave me an answer. Somehow He made me under-stand that a mother of toddlers just isn't like anyone else. Most of the time, my life was not under my own control at all, but more like a series of random events. It was in the way I responded to the events that my spiritual life could be measured. As when I handled Ben's indoor garden party so well. That wasn't me at all —so patient, so calm, such the good mother—but me stepping aside to let God respond as the perfect Father.

It isn't about a set-aside quiet time. It's about prayer that requires nothing more than a willingness to pray.

I was OK just the way I was, as long as I wasn't content to stay that way but willing to grow—to grow through pouring out my heart to Him and waiting for answers impressed without words on my heart. Finally, I understood it wasn't at all about a set-aside quiet time—especially at this season of my life—but more about prayer that required nothing other than my willingness to pray.

Victor Hugo, author of *Les Miserables*—my second favorite book after the Bible, and like the Bible a great tale of redemption[1]—once wrote, "There are moments when whatever the attitude of the body, the soul is on its knees." My soul was truly on its knees that day as I wailed to the Lord. I was in a desperate way. Yet that day I learned I didn't have to wait for desperation for my soul to kneel.

And so my laundry room became my prayer closet. For years it's been the place I meet the Lord each morning before my children awake, and at intervals throughout the day as I transfer clothes from baskets to washer, from washer to dryer, from dryer to baskets again. In those 12- and 20-minute snatches, I found my quiet time.

I never have any trouble finding God in my laundry room. He is always ready to receive my praise, my thanks, my prayers for family and friends, my joys and heartaches too.

My son Jonathan—now 11—was born with Down syndrome.[2] That wasn't a heartache, but a joy. When they placed him in my arms, I thought, *God must love me so much to give me such a special son.* I can't explain the confidence I felt, except to say God must have prepared me somehow in advance. I had a sense that we were at the beginning of a great adventure, as though we'd been carried to the top of the roller coaster, with the most exciting part about to come.

But the joy was short-lived. After the first night of sweet bonding, all kinds of scary things began to happen as the doctors found all kinds of things wrong with Jonny's little body. I couldn't hold him without the help of two nurses who sorted through the bundle of tubes and cords and sensors to place him in my arms. He needed a complete blood transfusion. He needed oxygen. And finally he needed more—surgery to straighten out his twisted little bowels. I watched helplessly as they packed my technologically swaddled baby into a portable incubator for emergency transport to the big university hospital across the San Francisco Bay.

And the unthinkable happened: I walked out of the hospital with no baby.

Shattered and in shock, before driving across the bridge to join Jonathan, I stopped at home and did a load of laundry.

For three weeks, Tripp and I switched off, saying hello and good-bye twice a day, taking turns at the hospital with Jonny—so pale and limp and vulnerable—and at home with worried brothers and sisters. Friends, neighbors, and even people we barely knew brought meals, baby-sat, took all seven of our kids bowling and swimming. I never felt so loved and cared for—and never so exhausted.

One night I dragged myself home, feeling about ready to give up, and found two friends waiting to surprise me. I had to admit, as caught up as I was in the drama of our life, I never would have let them visit if they'd called and asked me—which is why they probably came unannounced, as good friends should do if they have to.

And, oh, it was so good to sit and let them make me laugh while Christine gave me a foot massage and Sandy peeled oranges and fed them to me section by section.

All of my life I'd been in charge of taking care of others. Now I was learning to surrender.

Through it all the only thing I kept up with was washing clothes. The truth is, my laundry room—with its reassuring routine and memories of mornings with God—had become the most comfortable place for me when I couldn't be with Jonny. People must have questioned my sanity when I staggered in from a sleepless night at the hospital and made a beeline for the laundry room. How could I explain what it had become?

And so our big adventure proved to be not what I'd expected but a crash course in becoming completely dependent on God and friends to see us through the tough times. At the same time, we were discovering in neonatal intensive care just how much tougher life could be. Some babies were worse off than Jonny. Some were dying. Some had no one by their sides. I felt like all my life I'd been clueless and unaware—and I knew I'd never be the same.

We brought Jonny home three weeks later on a sun-drenched Easter morning. I'd brought so many babies home before him, I guess I must have started taking it for granted. Jonny's homecoming—after weeks of worry—was unremarkable on the outside, but seemed a magnificent affair.

But then, Jonny's birth changed my perspective on so many things. Just as my moment of belief had marked the previous years *Before Christ* and the following years *After Christ*, now there was another set of eras: *Before Jonny* and *After Jonny*. Everything—the way I viewed others, my church, my community—was different. As though Jesus had spat on the ground and made mud and put it on my eyes and made me finally, truly see.

Jonny's medical problems didn't end that Easter. In fact, there would be 14 more months of heartache/joy cycles as he was hospitalized again and again. Through it all I tried to be the model Christian mother, relying on my laundry to help me keep my sanity.

We'd managed to string a few healthy months together and Jonny had just celebrated his first birthday when sister Madeleine was born. A month later, Jonny was in intensive care, nearly dying of pneumonia, and now it was worse than ever, being split between two babies who needed me. Still, I hung in there, trying to be a good girl for God, keeping in mind what everyone kept telling me—God doesn't give us more than we can handle.

Oh, but He does!

Jonny'd been home only a few weeks and I'd only done two dozen loads of laundry before he was sick again. More rounds of lab work and X-rays, then a call from the doctor, "Bring him to the hospital right away. He needs another operation."

Enough! Now I'd really had enough. Sick of being the perfect long-suffering Christian mother, angry at God for not rewarding my good behavior, like a tantrumming toddler, I threw myself on the dining room carpet, banging the floor with my fists and raging: "Why, God? Why? What are You doing? I can't take it anymore!"

Ordinarily, I would have thought it wrong to be so disrespectful. I mean, He is God, after all. But these were extraordinary times and I was fed up. Fed up enough to stop acting the way I thought I should act and start acting real. How would God handle my eruption? Would I be punished? While I might have gotten away with whining on occasion, I'd never been angry with God. Was I allowed to be?

God sometimes gives us more than we can handle so we can learn to be totally dependent on Him.

God was bigger than my anger. He could handle it. I wasn't punished. In fact, after that operation followed by three weeks in the hospital, Jonny and I never went back again. His body was fixed for good.

Now I could see that contrary to popular belief—*God doesn't give you more than you can handle*—He does indeed sometimes give us more than we can handle, so we'll learn to truly rely on Him. Looking back, I think God was just waiting for me to let go and give Him the whole mess of Jonny's medical problems. He must have been as sick as I was of Barbara the Brave, Long-suffering Supermom. He must have delighted in hearing from Barbara the Angry-but-Real Frightened Little Girl.

Yet another lesson learned not during quiet time, but in real life—about what God expects from a believer. It isn't about where or when or how I pray. Instead, it's about realizing God is always there, whether I pray or don't pray. He's always ready to receive me.

It's not at all about prayer closets and quiet time—though they're nice if you've got the lifestyle to allow you the luxury. But for workaday moms like me, it's about getting real with Him, staying real with Him on a minute-by-minute basis. What God wants isn't my current version of what a faithful follower looks like, but an authentic relationship, where I don't hide who I am or how I feel.

This thing called prayer turned out to be not at all the way I first imagined—quiet moments with God in pastel places, like the atmosphere evoked in Thomas Kinkade paintings. Mine was more heavy brushstrokes like Van Gogh—or sharply angled like Picasso.

God wants an authentic relationship with you— a relationship where you don't hide who you are or how you feel.

I've never had the reputation of a "prayer warrior," for which I am grateful. I'm always glad not to be called on to pray in public—and have actually been known to say no when asked. I'd rather hear other people pray. I admire the cadence of self-confident prayers pounding like waves on heaven's shore or the quiet rhythm of praise pattering like raindrops on a leafy carpet.

My prayers aren't like that. They're full of starts and stammers and stops. Well-turned phrases are few and far between. While usually—as a writer, as a wife, mother, and friend—I'm trying to choose the best words to communicate clearly, with God it's different. I'm just desperate to communicate. If what comes out is confusion, He'll clear it up—like someone who helps me unlock the meaning of that Picasso painting.

What's most important: being real. And there's nothing like motherhood to bring out the real in a woman, is there?

Over the years, my prayers have changed. As a new believer, I turned to prayer when times were tough, when I was unhappy, when I needed answers. For a while, it was all about me—until I caught a clue I could pray for others, too, and probably should. So I prayed for my family and friends and then beyond to people I didn't really know—like people in the houses or children in the schools or shoppers in the malls I passed each day. I'd even pray for those I didn't want to pray for, like that driver who cut me off or the coach who yelled at my son or the friend who gossiped about me.

My prayer life grew a little richer when I latched on to this formula I learned somewhere:

Adoration

Confession

Thanksgiving

Supplication

Using this structure, I'd start by worshiping God and who He is. Then I'd call to mind and acknowledge my sins, asking for His forgiveness. Then I'd thank Him for my many blessings. Only at the end would I ask for anything I needed.

This was a good discipline. It gave me a firm foundation in not always thinking of myself. And once I overcame the limitations of being a "good" girl and praying just the right way—once I got real—it meant I'd probably cover all the bases in prayer, though not in such a structured way.

More and more, my prayer life became not just a compartment of my life, but part of me. From the early days praying in the laundry room, to the discovery of what it meant to get real with God, I realized that the limiting factor for my prayer life was only me—and the thoughts that cluttered my mind. I could choose to pray anywhere, anytime, while doing anything. All I had to do was turn my thoughts to God.

I've since discovered that this revelation—though very spontaneous and personal—was not unique. Some years ago, I came across a slim volume called *The Practice of the Presence of God,* a book that can be read in an hour and offers a lifetime of change.

In it, I found described what I as a busy mother had grabbed onto as a spiritual survival technique, described by a 17th-century French monk, Brother Lawrence, who taught himself to respond to God's presence at all times.

He wrote, "The time of business does not with me differ from the time of prayer, and in the noise and clatter of my kitchen . . . I possess God in as great tranquility as if I were upon my knees at the blessed sacrament."

And so we moms, too busy for quiet time and prayer closets, may find good company in this gentle soul. Housework doesn't have to be something that keeps us from prayer but something that brings us to prayer.

And it isn't just housework, it's whatever, wherever, whenever. So instead of listening to the radio, I can instead tune in to God. As Brother Lawrence says, "Lift up your heart to Him . . . the least little remembrance will always be acceptable to Him. You need not cry very loud; He is nearer to us than we are aware of."

Whenever I think of Him—and I'm constantly trying to increase the amount of time I spend thinking of Him—I thank Him for everything I can think of to thank Him for. I pray for Him to help me entrust the things I worry about to Him. I see the splendid trees, the Blue Ridge Mountains, the legendary Shenandoah River, or I hear a piece of music and thank Him for the abundance of beautiful forms with which He filled our world. I mean, as I remind my children all the time, He could have made only one kind of tree, only one kind of flower, only one cloud formation. We might have all looked the same or had the same voice. The world might just be black and white. The fact that the world is rich and full of variety constantly reminds me how much He loves us to surround us with such variety and beauty to make our imaginations soar.

It's that soaring imagination that every mother needs. It's that soaring imagination that makes it possible to be content as I fold the clothes and drive the car and stir the spaghetti sauce. It's that soaring imagination that lifts me out of the humdrum routine and helps me see my husband and children not as just the ones with the clothes habit that keeps me in the laundry room so many hours a day, but as the constantly unfolding miracles they truly are. It's the soaring imagination that keeps me mindful that even though the things I'm doing might not seem so important, in my Heavenly Father's eyes they always will be.

When I turn my thoughts to God, loading the dishwasher, sweeping the floor, getting up to nurse the baby at night, even changing a diaper can be a prayer. And as I turn my thoughts to Him, I pray for all the mommies like me who are too busy wiping peanut butter and jelly off little faces and kissing owies to maintain the practice of what the less encumbered call quiet time. I pray for mommies who can't remember how it feels to lie on the couch listening to the rain or reading a book, who can't grab five minutes in the shower without the world falling apart.

I know there are mommies whose prayer closets are buckets and scrub brushes, sewing baskets, garden patches, or car pools. And there are mommies who work outside the home whose prayer closets are assembly lines or switchboards or operating rooms. Everywhere are mommies squeezing moments of quiet time between customer calls or the clamor of kids.

I know this because now I understand that God is bigger than any place I set aside to meet Him and as near as I invite Him to be.

2

His Little Girl

I remember the day my dad left. He knelt on the sidewalk in front of our house and wrapped his arms around me. Then he said good-bye. The skimpy dress of a five-year-old girl couldn't protect me from the chill that gathered around my arms and legs. The scratchy whiskers against my cheek—would I feel them no more? The arms that felt so safe—would they be gone forever?

I needed those arms more than most, I think. So far the only thing stable about my life had been the presence of my parents. In five years we'd covered thousands of miles on the road moving from Kansas City, Kansas, to Fort Smith, Arkansas; from Arkansas to Rockford, Illinois; from Illinois to Atlanta, Georgia; from Georgia to Anchorage, Alaska; from Alaska to Long Beach, California.

No, my father wasn't in the service, though when I was young, I'd quickly answer yes when asked. Years later, as a political radical, I went the opposite way, actually bragging about what was really going on with my dad: when he ran up too many bills in one city, he'd move us on to the next. He always got away.

Did my mother understand what my dad's lack of character portended for her? Or was she taken by surprise when shortly after the birth of my second brother, my dad left her for another woman? She was excruciatingly naive, the 10th of 12 children from a poor but proud Irish family settled in Missouri. She'd married my dad at 19. In their pictures they look like a couple of movie stars. But didn't everyone in those days? Underneath the 1940s glamour of two heads of wavy hair, his pleated pants, and her high heels, they were really just two country bumpkins who struck out on their own.

Whether surprised or not by my dad's departure, my mom was devastated and unprepared. She moved us not too far to San Bernardino to live with my aunt and two cousins, parallel casualties of divorce.

Here is what I remember: the fig trees in the backyard and the wonderful cool beneath them. Also how much I hated figs and the smell of them rotting. My mother and aunt went off to work each day, leaving us with a housekeeper. Before they left they pressed a shiny, copper penny into the palm of each little hand, then turned the hand and kissed the back, leaving brilliant red lipstick imprints as a sort of pre-cell phone way of staying connected.

I went to a Catholic school, where they discovered I was smart. I skipped second grade—a good move academically but leaving me a social afterthought for the next 10 years.

Like Dorothy in *The Wizard of Oz*, "People come and go so suddenly here!" my life seemed just a series of random events that occurred without warning or explanation. Maybe it was because in the 1950s, kids were on a different footing with adults and parents didn't think we needed to understand. Or maybe my life was just different.

In any case, big changes always took me by surprise. As when my dad left five minutes after telling me. Or when my mother packed our suitcases and boarded our bedraggled little family on a train from California to Washington, D.C.

Did she and my aunt have a falling out? How did she muster up the courage for the trip? And how did she survive a week on a train with three little kids in tow? Trains were slower then, no air conditioning, no disposable diapers, and we were never candidates for first class.

On our arrival, another surprise: my mom said good-bye. She'd gotten a job, rented a small apartment in D.C., and arranged for us to live with a family way out in the country in Maryland.

Not a foster care situation through the state, but a private ar-rangement—like Cosette in *Les Miserables*—where my mother sent money for our board.

Was it at this point of being abandoned a second time that I made a decision not to feel? Or was it when our "foster family" turned out to be so cruel and abusive to the three of us and an-other brother and sister boarding there?

My mother found a boyfriend to drive her out for a visit every couple months or so—always so glamorous in a tight dress, heels, chunky costume jewelry, gloves, and big hat, I could hardly believe she was my mother. She'd bleached her hair blond, too, and she smelled like hairspray and cigarettes. She'd take pictures of her three children in front of a big wagon wheel sticking up by the driveway. Then she'd have her boyfriend take a picture of her with the kids. I was eight, my brothers five and two. Didn't she wonder why in the pictures we were never smiling?

Why couldn't I tell her what went on when she was gone? Any woman abused as a child will know why—because you just can't find the words.

I remember once in Alaska, my brother and I in the backseat of the car, bouncing around like peanuts as all kids did in those preseatbelt days. Suddenly, my brother pushed on the door han-dle. The door flew open and he fell out. It took my parents a few moments to notice, and we had traveled several hundred yards. My mother shook me, screaming, "Why didn't you tell us?"

Sometimes, for children, things are too awful to tell. My mother seemed so perfect on visiting days, I was afraid that if I told her it might break the spell, afraid she might never come back. Then, too, there was the fear that it was really all my fault. If my dad left, and my mother left, and these people didn't care for me either, there must be something wrong with me. The last thing I wanted was to draw my mother's attention to that.

We were rescued at the beginning of fourth grade, when my

mother said we could come home to live with her. And so I became a latchkey kid before there was a name for us. My brothers and I shared the bedroom, my mother slept on the couch. She worked as a clerk by day and a cocktail waitress at night. A neighbor watched my youngest brother, kept an eye on us after school, and tucked us in at night. It was lonely, but a relief from the foster home.

But my mother planned to send us back for the summer. As the end of the school year loomed ahead, I worried more and more. Finally, I got up the courage to write my mother a letter and put it on her pillow before I went to bed. That night I woke to find her crying on the foldout couch. She never acknowledged my clumsy confession, but the foster home was never mentioned again. That summer we were sent to stay with my Uncle Leo and Aunt Ginger and their eight kids in a bright, cheery three-story house in West Chester, Pennsylvania. It was a wonderful time of being part of a warm and loving family. And like a rainbow after a terrible storm, it filled me with hope and a promise of a brighter future.

But there would be many years before that hope and promise could be fulfilled.

Back for fifth grade with Mom, one fall day I walked home for lunch—as we city kids did in those days—only to find another surprise. My mom, who was usually at work, was home. And there was my father whom I hadn't seen or heard from in five years, ready to take me to live with him in Oklahoma City. My mother had already packed my suitcase. No time to even say good-bye to my brothers.

Later I was told my father had been asking to see us. My mother, on the verge of remarrying, struck a deal—he could have me if he'd stay out of my brothers' lives.

And so I ended up at 10 in my 11th home, with a new cast of characters: my father, 22-year-old stepmother, and their toddler son, ironically named after my father just like my first brother. My stepmother was less than thrilled to have a 10-year-old daughter thrust upon her. I tried to be helpful so she would like me more.

But I didn't see much of them. They both worked long hours, while someone watched the baby and I stayed home by myself. Now, without even my brothers, I was very lonely.

A year later, a sheriff showed up at our door with a notice re-asserting my mother's custody rights. I was placed on a plane—very much against my will as my father and stepmother had turned me completely against my mother—and flown back where I came from.

But enough.

Not everyone who loses a father will share the same story. But my life, with all its dramatic ups and downs, really emphasizes the vulnerability of children whose fathers abandon them. Despite the rosy picture painted for us in the media, growing up fatherless is just about the worst thing that can happen to a boy or a girl—even worse than losing a mother. Fatherless children are 4.6 times more likely to commit suicide, 6.6 times more likely to become teenaged mothers, 24.3 times more likely to run away, 6.6 times more likely to drop out of school, and 15.3 times more likely to end up in prison as teenagers. They are also 33 times more likely to be seriously abused and 73 times more likely to be killed.

None of these things happened to me, and yet my life took many turns it probably never would have. Shuffled here and there with or without my two brothers, I had an overwhelming sense of powerlessness, as though my life were some kind of Mr. Toad's Wild Ride, only not funny at all.

As far as needing sympathy—that's not where I'm going with this at all. What I really want to share is the enormity of the miracle that someone like me who grew up without a father could come to find the Heavenly Father and trust completely in His unconditional, unfailing love. The fact that it happened in an instant, that it wasn't something I studied or earned over time, that all it took was a simple statement of faith,[3] makes it for me as real as the chair I'm sitting on.

Regardless of how you grew up, you can trust completely in the Heavenly Father's unconditional, unfailing love.

Still, a lot happened in the years between my first 10 years and the last 16 years since I found the only true security. The Bible says, "Though my father and mother forsake me, the LORD will receive me" (Ps. 27:10). But I didn't know the Bible as a little girl, so I was left to find other ways to cope. In addition to the decision to stop feeling, I also decided this: *Don't depend on anyone and no one will disappoint you.*

Later, as an adult in counseling, I learned these decisions only became unhealthy once I had grown up and was on my own. For a child, they were simply survival techniques, helping me navigate the events of my childhood the way a child in a terrorist country learns to navigate the no-longer-safe streets of his town.

But what helped me survive childhood wreaked havoc in my adult years, as the cost of losing a father doesn't end when you grow up. There may be years of acting out, of making wrong decisions, adding layers to the scar—the glossy, too-tight skin formed over a deep wound. People see the outer toughness and don't realize how much hurt lies beneath. But I didn't know either.

By my 20s, I'd taken control of my future, acquired a good education, and showed great promise of rising above the pattern of my family's past. I guess you might say with no one to believe in, I learned to believe in myself.

Only when this unsustainable strategy dropped me down and out—and more alone than ever—did I finally face my fatherlessness.

So I was in my 30s when I sensed that what was missing was spiritual, and I finally launched a search for God. For someone like me the New Age movement held enormous appeal. Here I could wander into nooks and crannies, borrowing this and that to construct an image of God to mesh with my own deficiencies. Crippled by the lack of a real father in my life, seeing God only as some remote and impersonal force, my hope was that through understanding, I could appropriate the force—recognizing "God within me"—then manipulate it to find happiness.

With my eyes on the ground, happiness was as high as I could aim my sight. I wouldn't have thought to seek His love.

And yet how amazingly unconditional and enduring His love remained for me. No matter how I misunderstood Him, how well He continued to understand me. How patiently He waited as I wandered—for seven more years protecting me from harm, continuing to draw me nearer, gradually softening my heart.

No matter how we misunderstand God, He continues to understand and love us unconditionally.

My husband helped to soften me, though I never could have told him then. Watching him be a father to our children was like peeking through a frosted pane into a warm and cozy within. Although seeing my children experience a happy childhood was the next best thing to having one myself, how I wished sometimes to climb inside and receive that kind of love myself.

Oh, how ready I was the moment I first heard God was my Father! How easy it was to believe He loved me, had a plan for my life, and through Jesus Christ would have a relationship with me. Of course, I wanted a Father!

At last, I was someone's little girl! What a difference that has made in my life.

I have a Heavenly Father and He loves me! I may have gone through my childhood years feeling like no one thought I was special, but I know I'm special to Him. I may be a grown-up and older than I care to say, but I am and always will be His little girl. I can see myself at 57, 72, 93 still feeling like His little girl. I can see myself surrounded by those I love, saying good-bye, and knowing I'm going home to Daddy.

From the beginning of my walk with God, I've understood He was always there. It was never about Him not knowing me, but about me not knowing Him. Still, if my Heavenly Father loved me from the beginning—and I had a profound sense that He had—why did He let so much harm come to me? Fortunately, I found the answer very early on, in a place I would eventually learn had all the answers. I found it in the Bible.

I didn't grow up with the Bible, but after finding my way home to Jesus I couldn't rest until I'd read it cover to cover. So it didn't take long for me to get to the story of Joseph, at the end of Genesis—a story I'd never heard but the first one that grabbed me up as though God had whispered, "Barbara, this one's for you!"

Here was a child who was betrayed by those who'd been entrusted with his care. When his brothers sold him into slavery, he was absolutely powerless. He was taken far away and put to work in a strange place by his new owner, Potiphar. Like me, he was industrious. But after Potiphar matched Joseph's hard work with his trust, Joseph was betrayed again—this time by Potiphar's wife, angered by his refusal to betray his master and surrender his innocence to her.

Years in prison followed, where the Bible says, "the LORD was with him; he showed him kindness and granted him favor in the eyes of the prison warden" (39:21). When he interpreted the imprisoned cupbearer's dream—which promised restoration—Joseph asked the cupbearer to remember him when he was restored to Pharaoh's good graces. But the cupbearer forgot, and Joseph languished two more years in prison.

Only when the Pharaoh had a dream that no one could interpret did the cupbearer remember Joseph. Joseph's interpretation of that dream led Pharaoh to place him in the highest position he possibly could, second only to himself in ruling Egypt.

Flash forward to the famine Joseph predicted and his brothers coming to beg for food from a sibling grown beyond their recognition. Joseph deals with many emotions in his dealings with his first betrayers, until the dramatic scene at the end of Genesis.

His brothers then came and threw themselves down before him. "We are your slaves," they said. But Joseph said to them, "Don't be afraid. Am I in the place of God? You intended to harm me, but God intended it for good to accomplish what is now being done, the saving of many lives" *(50:18-20)*.

And so it was early on in my faith that I caught a glimpse that in the spiritual realm things are not always what they seem. My earthly life, like Joseph's, had been filled with abandonment, betrayal, and undeserved abuse. But it was those hurtful things that had in some way shaped me to become a woman poised to do the particular things God would reveal He wanted me to. I didn't have to be bitter, knowing that if I surrendered and let Him, God would use everything to make me better.

In the spiritual realm, things are not always what they seem. When we surrender to God, He can shape us into what He wants us to be.

In this way, I made peace with my past. Not an uneasy truce, but a real and permanent peace. I embraced each particular event, acknowledging that even if I had a choice, there's not one thing I would change.

In fact I've learned to count as blessings the things I never had:

I'm grateful for the full refrigerator we never had in my childhood, grateful for the meals we missed the last few days before my mother's paycheck. I'm grateful my tummy growled like an edgy animal. I hope I never forget it. Though the memory makes it exquisitely difficult to listen to my well-fed children complaining that they're starving an hour after a meal, it makes it extraordinarily easy to give some down-and-outer behind a cardboard sign enough to buy a meal—no strings or expectations attached.

I'm grateful for the nice house, the perfect family, the right clothes I never had. No matter where I live, how "together" my family is, or what I'm wearing now, there's almost no one I couldn't consider a friend. After years of never feeling good enough, I'd never do anything to make someone else feel that way.

I'm grateful for the stability I never had. Divorce, foster homes, frequent moves, and family separations were hard on me as a little girl, but blessed me with resiliency and endurance. More important, they gave me a heart for children.

The father I didn't have gives me the special privilege of having only one Father—"father to the fatherless" (Ps. 68:5). With no earthly model to shape my perception of God, I know for certain the love and warmth I feel from my Heavenly Father are real.

I'm grateful for the productive early adulthood I missed while, like a ricocheting pinball, I hit the dead ends of the counterculture. While, as a new Christian, I often wondered why God didn't help me reach Him sooner, I've learned that in God's economy, no time is wasted. My own "lost" years have made it easy for me to love my brothers and sisters still lost, to understand the emptiness that energizes them, to work a little harder at seeking common ground.

I'm grateful for the perfect wedding Tripp and I didn't have. Finding I was pregnant, we ran away and got married six days later—a miracle that takes my breath away. Neither of us had the wherewithal or character to make a commitment, and yet with the grace of a God we didn't yet know, somehow we did. Now Tripp says half-joking, "God pulled a shotgun wedding."

In God's economy, no time is wasted.

I'm grateful for our very imperfect marriage. As New Agers, Tripp believing wholeheartedly in his deity, and I believing in mine, living together was impossible, causing us to seek help at a Family Life marriage conference where we finally learned who Jesus really is and committed our lives to Him.

I'm grateful for the "perfect" baby we didn't have seven years ago. Anyone who's met Jonathan (number 8 of our 12) can see he is perfect just the way God made him—with an extra chromosome. He has opened parts of our hearts we never knew were there. I couldn't imagine having lived without him.

But now I couldn't imagine having lived without any of the parts of my life, even those that seemed unbearable as I was living through them. In fact, I have embraced every part—the good, the bad, and the downright ugly. For every part, I give thanks.

Some people blame their past for their shortcomings. But that's not what it's all about. That's being a victim—never a good place to be. And also far from understanding who God really is.

Here's what my experience has taught me: It's not the adversities in our lives that determine who we are—it's our response to them. When bad things happen, we can choose to be bitter or better. Like Joseph, we can trust that even when harm is intended, God will use it for good to accomplish His purpose in our lives.

Romans assures us, "And we know that in all things God works for the good of those who love him, who have been called according to his purpose" (8:28).

Lord, Please Meet Me in the Laundry Room

My first Bible study leader was a woman named Sandy. She had recently moved from Georgia to northern California with her husband and two daughters. Her house was unlike anything I'd ever seen, covered from floor to ceiling with heartwarming, whimsical stuff—the kind of stuff I see in all my neighbors' houses now that I live in Virginia. Cute southern knickknacks and doodads and things to keep your eyes busy.

I never see Sandy anymore, but I still love her dearly. So much of my walk with God was shaped by her, though she probably doesn't know. (Do you have someone in your life like that? Write and tell them today. It's only an accident that I get to put it in a book.)

Sandy was the friend who fed me orange sections one-by-one when I came home that night from being with Jonny at the hospital. She's also the one who greeted his birth with a card on which she drawled (Sandy's southern accent is so thick it came through in her writing): "Well, Barbara, I guess he'll never grow up to be president. But that's just as well." I loved that she could have a sense of humor and be so casual about something everyone else was walking on eggshells about. But also, since it was 1992, before the years of heavy presidential controversy, for years since the remembrance of that remark made me laugh out loud. It still does.

But it was a remark she made in 1987 that became a bedrock of my faith. It was at that first Bible study, the one where I was worried about my appearance, worried about my lack of knowledge, worried about my rose tattoo.

I can't remember what we were studying (and isn't that funny?), but the discussion turned to something so strange and foreign I thought I'd been transported into a science fiction discussion group. Our usually very placid Bible study was suddenly hijacked by words like pretrib and posttrib, and there was tension in the air. I looked to Sandy, our leader, to see what she would say.

"Well," Sandy drawled, placing her forearms on the table, parallel to the edge, one hand over the other, "I don't know the answers to those questions. . . . But God does, and that's good enough for me."

I decided then and there that if it was good enough for Sandy, it was good enough for me too. Ironically, years later Sandy entered seminary. That's not my path.

"Unless you change and become like little children, you will never enter the kingdom of heaven" (Matt. 18:3).

Though I once fancied myself an intellectual, and though I still enjoy learning and analyzing and discussing the things of the world, when it comes to believing, I keep it plain and simple. I am so content to be His little girl.

He is Jehovah Rapha, the God who heals, and my life is a demonstration of that power.

Is it not a miracle that someone who missed an earthly father's love can be healed to receive the love of the Heavenly Father? For that, I love Him more. He is Jehovah Rapha, the God who heals, and my life is a demonstration of that power.

The greatest privilege of all: to call Him *Abba, Father.*

According to Vine's *Word Dictionary*, "*Abba* is a word framed by the lips of infants and betokens unreasoning trust. *Father* expresses an intelligent apprehension of the relationship. The two together express the love and intelligent confidence of a child."

I remember once, before he left, my father carrying me home in his arms as blood gushed from a jagged cut on my foot. I was four and I was frightened, hoping that my father could take care of me. But though that day he bound and stopped the bleeding, no earthly father could have healed the wounded heart he later left behind. That hurt cried out for the love of a Heavenly Father.

And so I will always be His grateful little girl—trusting, dependent, and filled with faith in the arms that will never let me go.

3

Any Kind of Mother

"Honey, I'm just not that kind of mother," I said.

Jasmine, my seven-year-old Campbell-Soup-Kid-cheeked daughter, stopped her enthusiastic hopping up and down. Suddenly she looked very small.

She'd come home from school ready to burst with excitement, bouncing into the kitchen where I was making dinner to tell me about the big cake decorating contest at her upcoming school fair.

"Can we make a cake, Mom? Can we?"

A simple request for most moms. Not so simple for me. In 1983, making a cake for a cake contest posed such a challenge to my self-image and the way I'd conducted my first 13 years of motherhood, Jasmine might as well have asked me to climb Mount Everest.

"Honey, I'm just not that kind of mother," I said again with more *That's that* in my voice.

But though my voice was firm, inside I was squirming. There was something too familiar about this scene—something in the sadness of Jasmine's shoulders as she turned away, the resignation gathering like a heavy cloak around my little girl—that gave me pause. I began to wonder what it meant when I said I wasn't that kind of mom.

I thought of my own mom and her lack of involvement in my life. But what choice did she have? Abandoned with three young children, working two jobs to keep a roof over our heads, coming home exhausted long after we had gone to bed, she turned to booze to numb the pain. She had crazy, mixed-up relationships

39

with men. And so finally, between work and her problems with alcohol and men, there really wasn't much of Mama left. Clearly, she hadn't been the cake-making type.

Ironically, despite my best intentions not to, I came close to repeating her pattern, ending up at 20-something a divorced mother with two daughters and problems galore—problems with jobs, problems with drugs and alcohol, problems with men.

But in 1980, God began to reach for my heart, and my life began to change.

It started on March 17, when I woke up aching in my waterbed after another bleary night of heavy drinking and fell to my knees begging God to help me. I hadn't really been raised to think about God, much less to ask for His help. But somehow I suddenly realized the path I was on would lead to death, and in that split second I instinctively reached for the Giver of Life.

I don't know why it was that morning and none of the mornings before.

If there had been a believer in my life, perhaps I would have ended up at church. Instead I ended up at Alcoholics Anonymous, where I heard a lot of talk about a Higher Power and the need to surrender my life. This Higher Power was a very loosely defined "God as you understand Him," and there were even AA atheists who said that the group itself was their Higher Power. I barely noticed. For the first year of my sobriety, I was way too busy thinking about me to think much about God.

And yet, after a time, I couldn't deny the reality that my recovery was supernatural. Through the first 10 of AA's Twelve Steps, I learned to admit my powerlessness, to surrender, to be fearlessly honest with myself, to confess my faults promptly, and to seek forgiveness. AA taught me to live one day at a time, even—when times were particularly tough—from moment to moment. The Serenity Prayer helped:

Lord, grant me the serenity to accept the things I cannot change, the courage to change the things I can, and the wisdom to know the difference.

When I realized the path I was on would lead to death, I instinctively reached for the Giver of Life.

Without the numbing effects of drugs and alcohol, I also had to come to grips with how much like my mother I'd become, to recognize that in spite of my vows to do a better job I was still back at the starting line. My quest for freedom had prompted me to leave my first husband, who truly didn't deserve a runaway wife. And in my self-centeredness, I'd left my oldest daughter Samantha Sunshine as well. The truth was, I didn't want to be encumbered with an eight-year-old, while at two Jasmine Moondance was easy to drag wherever I went.

And boy did I drag her! From one San Francisco coffeehouse to the next, from party to party, from one weird situation to another. In the meantime, Samantha's dad took her to start a new life in Hawaii, only to return in less than a year with an ultimatum: either I take Samantha to live with me, or he would put her in a foster home.

We were sitting in a coffeehouse together when he told me, and the moment is engraved in my memory—deeply, as when the memory holds terrible sorrow together with the barest glimpse of hope.

A foster home. So it had come full circle. The little girl whose mother had once upon a time chosen her freedom over motherhood had now grown up and abandoned her own first little girl. The shock of realizing what I had done, that was the sorrow.

The glimpse of hope was this: I was able to perceive that abandoning her to her dad was one thing. But the threat of a foster home was something else. Still, I know what a selfish person I was then. It was only by the grace of God—the God I'd yet to meet—that I could not condemn my daughter to repeat that part of my unhappy past.

Some crazy years were yet to come, years when my behavior and choices put my girls at great risk. We lived in a second-story turn-of-the-century flat in the roughest part of San Francisco's Mission district, a place most of my friends were afraid to come visit. As a proud counterculture radical, I took pride in living among "the people." We saved our change and washed our clothes in the Laundromat across the street, next to the bar that played loud mariachi music all night, every night. Each day, Samantha walked three blocks to catch the public bus to go to school—alone. Having grown up in similar circumstances in Washington, D.C., it didn't occur to me that a good mother wouldn't let her child walk alone in the city.

But I wasn't a good mother, I know that now. I'm grateful God protected my daughters until I learned to be one.

Of course, I didn't understand this—how God had always been with me—until I'd been a believer for a while. Then, as though the veil was lifted between my prebelieving and believing selves, I came to understand that it wasn't just a question of when I came to know Him. He always knew me. He was always, always there. At critical moments He nudged me in a certain direction. And through many dark times in my life He was watching out for me, even to the point of saving my life when it might have been lost.

I didn't see those special moments all at once. It was as though when I became a believer God gave me a charm bracelet of faith, then added charms as we went along. I'd remember something from the past and see it suddenly revealed for what it was—a time when God showed His love for me before I had learned to love Him. Like the time in 1958 when my mother sent us to my uncle's instead of the foster home, or in 1978 when I chose not to let Samantha go, or the years in San Francisco when God kept us safe from harm, or the time in 1980 when I finally called out to God to help—though it would still be seven years before I came to really know Him.

During those seven years, God was with me and helped me as I began moving my life more determinedly in a certain direction—that of becoming the mother He wanted me to be. AA taught me to be fearless about facing the mistakes I'd made and eager to apologize to people I'd hurt, including my girls.

In the process I learned to get real.

I remember several months into my sobriety thinking, "I don't even know how to be a mother!" And that was the truth—I didn't know at all. Without a loving and nurturing relationship with my own mother, I didn't know where to begin as a mother myself.

When Samantha was a toddler, I'd trained to become a Montessori teacher.[4] There was indeed a part of me that loved children and wanted to help them, and I'd taught in Washington, D.C., and San Francisco. But being a mother was different from being a teacher. And though I spent time with my girls—not stinting on trips to the beach, the zoo, or the movies—sometimes it somehow felt like there were missing pieces.

To find them, I'd walk a couple blocks to the neighborhood park—by the time I got sober we had moved north of San Francisco to Marin County—and park myself on a bench to watch the mothers and children there. Written on my heart are these lessons from people I never knew: the unwavering gaze, the tender touch, the patient smile, kisses and hugs galore. Yes, I saw bad parenting too, but that only underscored the beauty of the moms who knew how to love and nurture.

Admitting I wasn't the mother I could be was the first step to becoming one. But really, I was only taking baby steps. There was so much to take care of that first year. There were the practical things like learning to pay my bills on time, to grocery shop before the refrigerator was empty, to go to the filling station before my car ran out of gas. But there was also the more difficult challenge of learning to deal with emotional crises without resorting to pills or booze. In many ways, I was only 16 emotionally—the age when I first found alcohol offered an escape. Now I had to face the problems I'd been putting off for years—had to face them on my own, but without the maturity or wisdom of a normal 30-something.

And so it was that after a year of sobriety, I woke up one morning and called in sick to work. Really, I was just too depressed to get out of bed. I wanted to pull the covers over my head and never move. Odd, because besides making progress as a mother, I'd found great happiness in going back to work as a Montessori teacher.

By noon, I had diagnosed my problem and written my own prescription: There was a spiritual vacuum in my life. I needed to find out more about this Higher Power that had been helping me through the past year. My first step was to visit a more mature AA sister who had a reputation for being spiritual. She was kind and understanding and sent me away with an armload of books to get me started on my journey to find God.

And so I stumbled into the New Age—a vast smorgasbord of spiritual ideas where I was invited to taste and blend whatever offerings appealed to me. I learned about the God within me and creating my own reality, about past lives that explained the karma that I'd had to work out in my early years. I learned to meditate and use affirmations to remain free of anxiety.

And then, the greatest thrill of all—I met a man on the same spiritual wavelength. We began meditating and reading our spiritual devotions together. We were also sleeping together—after all, with no moral background we didn't know any better. By then

I'd been sober for two years; Tripp had been sober one. He was six years my junior, never married. He was crazy about my girls—and while Samantha was a little aloof, Jasmine was crazy about him. I was crazy about Tripp too—and still am.

We planned on getting married eventually, but as Tripp jokes now, "God pulled a shotgun wedding." Three months after our first date—on December 26—I rolled up my sleeve for a blood test (the way it was done way back when) and learned six hours later I was pregnant. That night I told Tripp.

"Well, we'll have to get married!" he said.

And so, on January 2, 1983, we were married at sunset on the deck of an inn overlooking the Pacific Ocean at Jenner-by-the-Sea, California. The only people in attendance were our friends Danny and Debbie, another crazy, mixed-up unmarried AA couple (who much, much later became Christians). Debbie made my bouquet from flowers she picked by the road, our vows were a New Age mishmash I can't remember at all, and our wedding cake was a leftover blueberry pie.

But our marriage was real, as God has since revealed. He wanted us together because it was as a couple we would finally find Him. And our marriage was based on two miracles.

The first was that I was fertile at all. During my wild and crazy days, I'd had an infection so bad the on-call surgeon had come close to removing my reproductive system. Instead, he opted for two weeks of IVs in the hospital and a couple months of bed rest.

"But," he said ominously, "you'll probably never be able to have children again."

"Yippee!" I thought, being the "liberated," wrongheaded young woman I was. But just to be on the safe side, I used my diaphragm religiously. So how did I end up pregnant?

The second miracle was even more profound: we didn't get an abortion. Besides my lack of religion, I was a radical feminist who had fought for abortion rights, even had an abortion myself;

Tripp had been through two with another girlfriend. Like other nonbelievers out of touch with the sanctity of life, we would tend to shrug off abortion as an inconvenience comparable to a root canal—no moral consequences or emotional aftermath.

That the thought of abortion never entered our minds, that we didn't just drift along through the pregnancy waiting till whenever to get married, really impresses me with God's mercy and love. Looking back, I feel as though He gave us tunnel vision and a sense of urgency so that despite numerous dire warnings from family and friends and despite our own base natures, we were married within a week.

God had a plan. Our marriage was part of that. Another charm I'd eventually discover on my bracelet of faith.

And now here I was, a stay-at-home mom, each morning kissing my husband good-bye for work and my daughters good-bye for school. In anticipation of the new baby, we'd rented a bigger house on a hill with a deck overlooking the hills and valleys of Marin. I kept myself busy wallpapering and rearranging furniture.

This was a new kind of life for me, being a real stay-at-home mom. Before Samantha's first birthday, I'd become a radical feminist, plopped my daughter in day care and gone back to college to pursue my dream of becoming a Montessori teacher. I'd always looked down on women who were "only housewives," yet now here I was "only a housewife" myself. And I found I liked it immensely! Liked having something other than myself to live for. I didn't mind the housework. I loved being home when my girls came in from school. I was happy to have time to try new things to cook. I felt so happy with my life, I'd have to pinch myself to believe it. I was a different woman, indeed.

But God knew I had a lot more growing to do.

"Honey, I'm just not that kind of mother," I'd answered Jasmine automatically when she came home that day, but the words seemed to ricochet like pinballs through all the nooks and crannies of my mind, shaking up enough dust to spark the mother of all mental sneezes. Obviously some clutter needed clearing.

There was the clutter of my feminist politics, which caused me to look down on "womanly" pursuits like cooking, sewing, volunteering at school. And there was the clutter of my own childhood, my own relationship with my mom, which kept me from seeing all that motherhood could be.

Suddenly, I realized that every opinion I held on motherhood was up for grabs. It was a spiritual awakening of sorts—not the one yet to come when Tripp and I found Jesus, but a smaller one. While I wasn't yet a new creation in Christ (2 Cor. 5:17), God must not have wanted to wait four more years for me to become a better mother.

And so somehow my thoughts were lifted higher to receive this inspiration: that there were no limits or boundaries to my motherhood, that I could become any kind of mother I wanted to be. That discovery made all the difference in the world in the next 20 years of my mothering—and probably the rest of my life.

But it all started with a little girl who wanted her mother to make a cake.

I took her hand and brushed her curls away from her eyes. "Well, maybe we could give it a try," I said, tentatively.

But when I saw Jasmine's shoulders lift and the hope return to her eyes, sense of purpose grew.

"What kind of cake were you thinking of?" I asked, hoping it would be something I could actually do. I've just never been a creative person at all.

She wanted Garfield, the orange cartoon cat with the mischievous eyes and the ear-to-ear grin. She produced a picture from Sunday's comics and we set to work, our kitchen becoming a flurry of cake mix, frosting, and orange coconut until at last a Garfield—nearly perfect, if I had to say so myself—sat smugly on a foil-wrapped board, just waiting to take his prize.

Tripp, sensing some significance, grabbed the camera and took a picture—a picture I treasure to this day.

There are no limits or boundaries to the kind of mother you can be.

The next morning, Jasmine and I proudly carried our Garfield cake into her classroom. There, my pride in my accomplishment was quickly cut to size when I saw the other entries, which included a three dimensional playground, an aerial model of the school, a baseball diamond with game in progress, and a five-car train. I stifled a twinge of inadequacy by reminding myself that other mothers had racked up much more experience than my 24 hours.

That we won fifth place in second grade tells me it must have been almost impossible to walk away without an award. Yet for me—someone who never used to do stuff like that for my daughters—it was good as Olympic gold. And for Jasmine—whose mommy had finally woken up to smell the coffee—it was priceless.

I still have the certificate we won that day, and I keep it and the picture of the cake to remind me not to say no without thinking. Since then, God's asked me to do some unusual things, and it's been a joy to be able to say, "Yes, Lord, I'll do that. It's not familiar territory at all, but I'm willing to go there if You'll hold my hand."

In that way I've learned obedience. And I've also seen it carried down the line to the next generation. For instance, when Samantha complained a couple springtimes ago that she thought God was calling her to begin homeschooling her four sons, who were then in Christian school. I'd homeschooled many of my children for many years by then, but never put any pressure on her to follow in my footsteps.[5]

"I just don't understand why. They're doing really well at school. And I really don't want to do it," she said.

"Well, if God really wants you to do it, He'll give you the willingness," I said.

A week went by and she called: "Mom, I've been checking out the curricula and I'm so excited about homeschooling! But I'm going to wait till summer vacation to tell Timmy, because he'll be upset about leaving his friends."

Another week went by. Then, "Guess what, Mom? Timmy told me he wants to be homeschooled next year!"

Don't you love how God does that? I've heard it said that God doesn't call the equipped but equips the called. Samantha's experience is a vivid reminder to me of my own. God called me to be a mother even though I wasn't prepared at all. But my years in AA taught me to be teachable, and my Garfield cake experience taught me to always think outside the box. And my love for God and gratitude for how He'd rescued me gave me the willingness to listen to the specific things He wanted to tell me.

I love the story of how Elijah waited on the mountain for the Lord to pass by:

> Then a great and powerful wind tore the mountains apart and shattered the rocks before the LORD, but the LORD was not in the wind. After the wind there was an earthquake, but the LORD was not in the earthquake. After the earthquake came a fire, but the LORD was not in the fire. After the fire came a gentle whisper (1 Kings 19:11-12).

For someone like me whose life for many years seemed consumed with all kinds of commotion, to hear the gentle whisper —or, as the King James says, *the still small voice*—is a miracle and a relief. Only a few times have I heard actual words as we know them, but God doesn't need to use earthly words to impress my heart with things He wants me to understand. He uses a still small voice.

God doesn't call the equipped.
He equips the called.

It was the voice that called Samuel (1 Sam. 3) while he lay in bed. The voice called him quietly and simply—called him by name. At first Samuel didn't know the voice and went to Eli, the priest in whose service he was. Three times the voice called Samuel's name, and three times Samuel answered his earthly authority. Then Eli understood who was really calling and told Samuel how to answer the Lord: "Speak, LORD, for your servant is listening" (v. 9). And God spoke to Him.

Just as I want to be practicing His presence as many moments a day as I can, I want my heart to be like Samuel's, turned to God and whispering, "Speak, for Your servant is listening."

God, Your servant Barbara is listening! Listening for Your direction this day. Listening for Your wisdom in dealing with a wayward child. Listening for Your patience when I've lost my own. Listening for Your comfort when I'm tired or depressed. Listening for Your assurance that I needn't compare myself to others. Listening for Your encouragement as I encourage other mothers. Listening for anything that will help me become more conformed to Christ.

You'd think by now, with 12 kids, 8 grandchildren, and 34 years of practice I might not need to listen so hard, but I do. For there are days I seem to barely get through. But then there are days my spirit soars on wings like eagles, when I can run after my kids and not grow weary, when I can walk miles just cleaning up my house and not be faint (a mother's paraphrase of Isa. 40:31).

What makes the difference? I guess it's whether or not I'm really listening, whether I'm really ready to let God lead. Knowing God as Abba Father, it seems natural to put my hand in His and let Him lead me where He wants me to go, but some days I'm better at it than others.

I remember in the movie *Chariots of Fire,* when Eric Lidell's sister scolds him for choosing running over missionary work. Eric listens respectfully and agrees that his desire to run makes no sense at all, adding, "I just know that when I run I feel His pleasure."

I want to feel God's pleasure too. That means I will listen for His guidance on the big issues and small ones too.

Sometimes that means going against the advice of friends, as when we moved to a rural community and after years of home-schooling felt led to enroll our children in public school. Since then, we've listened for guidance each year for each child. Had I decided I would homeschool everyone for 12 years, or had I decided I'd never homeschool at all—had I made up my own mind, how could I have heard what God would have me do?

Sometimes it means unique ways of handling family matters. Here's an example: Following cultural tradition, Tripp and I might have been ashamed that our first son was born less than nine months after our marriage. We might have fudged on dates or made it a taboo subject. However, we've since been redeemed and forgiven, and we know God used my pregnancy to nudge us into a commitment that would eventually lead us to Him, so we actually make it a point on Joshua's birthday to recount God's miracles with our family. In fact three sons would be born before Tripp and I came to believe, three sons whose names speak of belief. Their names—Joshua Gabriel, Matthew Raphael, and Benjamin Michael —like fingerprints all over the first four years of our marriage, reveal that though we didn't know it, God was always with us.

And God had plans for us as parents. Today, Tripp and I have 12 children, including 4 boys with Down syndrome—1 by birth and 3 by adoption. Samantha and her high school sweetheart/now husband, Kip, have 5 children. Jasmine and her husband, Nathan, have 3. Our family is close—so close that when Tripp and I moved the 10 children still at home from California to Virginia last year, both married daughters and their families followed. The 24 of us spend every Sunday together. God's given us more responsibility than most, but I can't stop rejoicing that though I didn't deserve it, He gave me a second chance at motherhood.

Knowing God as Abba Father, it seems natural to put my hand in His and let Him lead me where He wants me to go.

God's plan for my life couldn't be fulfilled when I was a woman who could say in all seriousness, "I'm not that kind of mother." He needed a mother who was willing to take an honest look at herself, to refuse to accept the limitations of the past, to take risks, to stretch and grow, even to throw off the concept of being like all the other mothers in order to become the kind of mother He wanted me to be.

4

A Mommy's Life for Me

"Are those all your children?"

At the doctor's office or the zoo, in grocery aisles or church parking lots, for years I've caught this question in every tone imaginable—from amusement to alarm.

OK, I admit it. En masse, our family can be a little unsettling, even when we've left a few behind. Then it's even more fun, because I can say, "No, it's not all of them—a few had other things to do."

This usually throws 'em for a loop—when they meant *Are those all **your** children?* and I answer as if they asked *Are those **all** your children?"*

"How many do you have?"

"Twelve."

Eyes pop, jaws drop, and then—unless I'm dealing with an overpopulation fanatic[6]—the conversation takes off. In this way, over the years, I've met enough people to populate a small town. Big families stimulate the curiosity of even the most socially cautious. Folks want to know whether they're all our own (though three are adopted, they're still our own!), if we've figured out where they come from, and when we'll be finished.

Some want to share their own stories of growing up in a big family, their spouse's big family, or the big family that lived down the street. Big smiles, sweet memories—then maybe a nostalgic sigh: "Yeah, you just don't see big families that much anymore."

In some parts of the country, that's truer than others. I know because we spent many years bringing up our big family in northern California, where it's popular to remain "child free," and those souls brave enough to commit to children most often opt for one or two. Things are different here in northern Virginia, where families with children outnumbering parents are absolutely the norm.

Still, there aren't nearly the number of megafamilies there used to be.

Sometimes I feel like a fossil. Indeed, in this age of sensible family planning, some people seem to regard me as one who might unlock a few mysteries. "Why do you have so many?" some want to know. With reverence, others ask, "How do you manage?"

How indeed? Believe me, even those blessed with such prodigious progeny find it sometimes staggering to contemplate.

Good thing we don't have much time to think.

Instead, most likely, we're busy every minute of every day, struggling with several sets of shoelaces or six loads of laundry, engaged in an interminable battle with clutter, and cooking in pots fit for the army who fights it. We're driving to endless rehearsals, lessons, games, and haircuts. We're taking children to dozens and dozens of medical and dental checkups a year. And on Sundays we're buckling a maxi-wagon full of seatbelts and shuttling what often feels to us like a cast of thousands into their various niches at church.

In other words, we're doing the same thing every other family does, only in jumbo amounts.

People always say, "Oh, you must be so organized!"

Well, yes, that's true—but only because I have to be. A mother of many is a lot like the CEO of a company—she has no choice but to run a tight ship. She must be able to delegate and inspire. She must know how to admonish and when to encourage. She has to have the big picture, yet be responsible for the details—the buck stops at her countertop. In fact, I've often thought that if they ever understood what makes megamoms tick, corporate headhunters would be beating down our doors to take the helm of some poor, struggling, heretofore-mismanaged company. Before too long, a megamom would make the cover of *Fortune* magazine—and then, who knows?—maybe *Time*'s Person of the Year.

Yeah, well, anyway—it doesn't hurt to dream.

On a more realistic level, no matter how organized she is, a megamom can't expect things to run smoothly for long—what with trips to the emergency room, suddenly plummeting grades, teen heartbreaks, and orthodontics. I don't think there's ever been a time when all our children were in crisis at the same time, but Tripp and I have sometimes felt spread pretty thin. Sometimes we're responding so fast, it all becomes a blur. Then I think of having many children as being like the carnival game Whack-a-Mole. You know, the one where the moles pop up in a maddeningly irregular sequence, and your job is to whack each with a hammer—fast, because the object of the game is to whack as many as possible. In this way, a megamom learns to spot and respond to crises quickly, hoping to whack them back before they're full-blown.

It's simply a matter of survival.

Come to think of it, though, don't all mothers feel the same —the CEO syndrome or the Whack-a-Mole frenzy? Aren't we all in some stage of learning to beat the pressure?

And don't we sometimes feel discouraged and underappreciated? I mean, unlike the corporate CEO, we don't get a lot of glory for a job well done. And even if we beat the game of Whack-a-Mole, no one rings a bell and gives us a gigantic stuffed animal.

A mother's transcendent moments can be few and far between.

Sure, as a megamom with Montessori training, I've got lots of ideas about making family life more manageable—and I've written books and articles and taught workshops to share them.

But *this* book is about more than teaching children to be self-reliant, orderly, and helpful. Because even if her children are the most self-reliant, orderly, and helpful children in the world, a mother who's not finding joy in her daily life with them needs to know she can.

I found the joy when I surrendered.

The real surrendering process began in 1987, four years after the Garfield cake, when Tripp and I had reached an impasse in our marriage. Our New Age religion, which seemed to be working in every other area of our life together, was falling flat when it came to our marriage. Having nothing to start with, together we'd built a successful business, bought a beautiful home in a county where we shouldn't have been able to afford one (another charm on the faith bracelet!), and contributed to charities. With the addition of three sons, we now had five healthy children. We enjoyed a reputation in the community as a wholesome, happy, successful family.

But there was a flaw in this picture of perfection. When it came to spiritual matters, Tripp and I were in agreement. About everything else—our business, raising children, in-laws, finances —we never could agree.

So even though friends flocked to us for spiritual advice, once we waved good-bye and closed the door, Tripp and I were left with just each other and the sad state of our relationship. The arguing, stubbornness, and lack of trust hung like fetters around our marriage. For the second time, I was ready to break free.

Before I could take any action, God intervened. And it was in a highly unusual way since we lived in such a highly unusual place.

In Marin County, California, just north of San Francisco, only 4 percent of the population attends church. Like everyone else around me, I held Christianity in contempt, judging it inferior to the more "sophisticated" spiritual practices Tripp and I were following.

With no believers around to deliver the truth about why our

marriage wasn't working, God used the radio to get us to the place where someone could tell us.

The way had been prepared when driving Josh to Montessori school one morning, spinning the dial between music and news, I'd come across a man's voice filled with kindness. His words were full of wisdom about parenting, which I needed since I was still trying my best to learn to be the perfect mother. In this way, I'd become addicted to Dr. James Dobson in the morning. In those early days there was little political content to Focus on the Family. That was a good thing for me, because that would have turned me away from the voice I needed to steer me toward the real Voice I needed to hear.

One morning Tripp and I had had another bitter fight before I left, and I was fuming as I shoved Josh in his car seat and began the 10-minute drive to his school.

"This is it! I've had it! He has to go!" I thought, about to make Tripp another ex.

Automatically, I flipped on the radio only to find that soothing, fatherly voice talking about rebuilding marriages. Dr. Dobson's guests that day were Dennis and Barbara Rainey, whose *Weekend to Remember* marriage conference was being held in San Francisco the next weekend. They said it strengthened—sometimes even saved—marriages.

In a last-ditch effort, I signed us up.

Tripp and I had a major argument that Friday afternoon and exchanged many angry words on our way to the conference. But by some miracle—God surely has never spared them on us—we did not turn back.

At the first night's session we sat in a room with 600 people, listening to and laughing with the speakers whose talks kept coming back to help us fill in the blanks in our marriage workbooks. We went over the world's plan for marriage, which meant a 50/50 relationship, selfishness, and difficult adjustments. We learned that God has a very different plan for marriage.

The next day we learned that God loves us and has a plan for our individual lives as well. This was the first of what they called the Four Spiritual Laws.[7] The idea that God cared for us personally was a radical departure from the vague, impersonal religion we had been practicing.

I was all ears for the rest, which described how sin had separated us from God, how God sent His Son to bridge the gap, and how we could receive Jesus Christ to know and experience God's plan.

I had never heard anything like this before. Jesus was more than just another spiritual teacher! I prayed silently, confessing that I was a sinner and asking Jesus to become my Lord and Savior. Through my tears, I looked at Tripp. He was crying too.

We came home as different people. With no previous exposure to Christianity, we were not sure what had happened to us. But we knew something had changed.

What had changed was this: though God had been able to nudge our lives in a certain direction here and there before—as when I got sober or Tripp and I got married or I became willing to be a better mother—now we knew the still, small voice was whispering wordlessly to us all the time.

In *The Weight and the Glory*, C. S. Lewis says, "I believe in Christianity as I believe the sun has risen. Not only because I see it, but because I see everything by it." Certainly for Tripp and me, the world was now a different place.

We began to read the Bible, and through reading learned that we had been born again (John 3:3). By the time we realized that meant we needed to go to church with other believers, no one needed to tell us to get rid of our New Age books and tapes, our pictures and idols. No one needed to tell us our former beliefs in astrology, reincarnation, and pantheism were not true.

God already had.

"What are they into now?" our children, our parents, and our

Though God had nudged us in a certain direction here and there before, now we knew the still, small voice whispering to us wordlessly all the time.

friends asked. Yet as they saw our relationship being healed, their hearts softened. One by one, our children put their faith in Jesus. Day by day we learned of God's care for us as He healed our wounds from the past and blessed our family with love and peace.

And so I learned the sweetness of surrender—that I could put my life in the hands of a loving Father and expect that the outcome would be good, that if I stopped living for me and started living for Him, my life would be filled with joy.

I guess I could have surrendered my life to Christ and secured my salvation and come home and continued living for me. But after so many years of living without God, I was so grateful to experience His love, I really wanted to live for Him. This has meant going beyond simple obedience by actually surrendering each moment to Him.

Not that I've always been perfectly on target, but since 1987 my life has been governed by the revelation that surrender doesn't mean defeat over anything but my own selfishness. And as my selfishness is defeated, my capacity for joy is fulfilled.

Here's what I mean:

1 Sam. 15:22 says, "To obey is better than sacrifice." But surrender is better than both. To do the right thing *in the right spirit* —that's what it's really all about.

Surrender doesn't mean saying, *OK, if I have to,* then gritting my teeth and clenching my fists and willing myself to be obedient. As a mom, I have so many things that elicit that response— things like muddy shoes and dirty bathtubs and getting up in the middle of the night to change a wet bed.

And I could go through the motions and do them without ever saying *Yes!* I could do them and be bitter, not better. I could be obedient and never feel God's pleasure.

Surrendering means saying yes with a smile, actively embracing whatever life sends my way each day and each night. *Yes, God, I'll do that!*

One of the most important things I've learned is this: There are the big events in life and the big choices—*Will we get married, will we move or will we stay, how many children, will I work or will I stay home?*

But most of life is lived in between, in the little things. And most of these things you can't change. You can't change the last 30 minutes in which your toddler scribbled all over the wall with permanent marker or how many poopy diapers your kids will have this week.

As a wife and mother, you have a lot you could feel discouraged, frustrated, depressed, maybe even resentful or bitter about. Each of us, no matter how good our intentions, has these moments. God hasn't given me the task of writing books because I do these things perfectly but because I've thought about them and tried to live them.

The important thing to know is that it is our choice how we feel about what we do. I can't change a lot of the circumstances of my life, but I can change my attitude. I can decide to fall in love with what I do—no matter how difficult it seems. And when God asks a little extra of me, I can say *Yes!*

A year after Jonny's birth, Madeleine was born. Since Jonny's development was delayed, they grew up like twins—babbling, playing, taking their first steps together. But we knew it wouldn't be long before Maddy's progress would outstrip her brother's (still, to this day, they're close like twins, though—always looking out for the other). Tripp and I felt led to adopt another baby with Down syndrome to grow up with Jonny. And so we ended up in

1995 with our 10th child, Jesse Mateo. We thought that would be the end of it, until in 1996 we were asked to adopt Daniel, and then in 2000 Justin.

People tell me, *Oh, I could never do what you do . . . you are so patient.* Really, I am no one special. I'm just a woman who has learned to say yes to God, a woman who's learned how to surrender.

But when I think back to the beginning, there were some things it took me quite a while to surrender to—things like not expecting my house to look perfect and not expecting to sleep through the night.

That's why I can tell you from experience that the sooner you surrender, the happier you'll be.

Today you might be tired because someone was up all night with an earache. You might be looking at four loads of laundry and the dryer just broke and Sears can't come out until Thursday. Your hyperactive daughter may be whining because she's hungry even though you just finished breakfast 37 and a half minutes ago. The phone is ringing and you wanted the answering machine to get it, but your son is bringing it to you proudly and it is on. Someone has a poopy diaper (at what point in our lives can we stop saying the word *poopy*?). There are dirty socks on the kitchen counter. (You mothers of preschoolers need to know that no matter what kind of godly home you have, no matter how tastefully decorated, no matter how firm your rules, it is a genetic thing with boys that they shed rolled up socks all day all over the house. If you have more than one boy, of course, you can never identify who the particular shedder of each pair is, but no matter who picks them up, your laundry time is increased 50 percent because of having to unroll each little sock ball before inserting it in the machine.) You need to go to the grocery store, but the baby's asleep, but by the time the baby wakes up, your husband will be home expecting dinner. Do you dare serve him fish sticks again?

Yeah, I have those days too.

To prepare for them, I psyche myself up for a day of mothering by blasting Steven Curtis Chapman's "Great Adventure":

> *Saddle up your horses, we've got a trail to blaze*
> *Through the wild blue yonder of God's amazing grace.*
> *Let's follow our leader into the glorious unknown.*
> *This is a life like no other—this is the Great Adventure.*

I doubt if Steven Curtis Chapman was thinking about a mother's life when he wrote those lines, but I find them absolutely applicable, don't you? It is a life like no other. It is a glorious unknown, a wild blue yonder of God's amazing grace.

Motherhood is our great adventure—the opportunity God has given us especially to learn the lessons He wants us to learn. When I'm distracted during the day from that purpose, just reminding myself can make me smile.

Emily Dickinson said, "The soul should stand ajar, waiting for the ecstatic experience." I may not be able to write poetry like she did, but I can sure relate. Motherhood has a way of keeping my soul standing ajar. Having oodles of children can lead to lots of mistakes and messes, but it can also lead to miracles and merriment. I just need to be ready for them, take the time to enjoy them thoroughly, and remember to give thanks for these little reminders to stop taking things so seriously and to have more fun with the job God has given me.

Last year, our family moved to Virginia—a homecoming I never expected when I left with Samantha in 1972 to find out more about "California Dreamin'." In those days, as a member of the counterculture, I hated America and all it stood for. I thumbed my nose at courtesy and tradition. In San Francisco and Marin County, I felt very much at home, surrounded by people of the same persuasion. But when God broke through my darkness and I began to see everything by His light, everything was different. Trying to raise good children in a culture created by people like me was suddenly like swimming upstream—and then some. Parents in Marin rejected school dress codes because rules would impinge on their kids' freedom. Teens were expected to have sex and no one better make them feel guilty about it. So, here I was, an extremist-come-lately who wouldn't allow her kids to see R-rated movies or swear.

You can imagine. Or if not, your children are all still young and you will eventually be able to imagine very well.

So, like the prodigal son, I was reminded that there was a better place—and it was a place I knew well. For 10 years, Tripp and I tried to sell our home and business to move east, but it didn't happen until 2002—just in the nick of time, as by 2003, California dreamin' had turned into a nightmare.

Motherhood is our great adventure—the opportunity God has given us especially to learn the lessons He wants us to learn.

We traveled that summer from California to Virginia—3,000 miles with 10 kids in 8 days. Two months later, Jasmine and her husband, Nathan, and their 3 children moved here too, followed shortly by Samantha, Kip, and their 5. In that monumental move —a weird reversal of Horace Greeley's "Go West, young man!" to "Go East, old woman!"—the future of our family was radically changed. It's awe-inspiring to think that Samantha and I left in 1972 to return 30 years later with 22 native Californians—and that somehow that is part of God's plan for each of us and our family as a whole.

But the story of our move to Virginia is just a setup for the story I have to tell about an ecstatic-in-a-motherhood-sort-of-way experience I had a few months after moving here.

Coming from California, my children had their first introduction to the four seasons. They'd grown up with only two: some rain for six months, no rain at all for six months. In Virginia, they made the acquaintance of humidity, spontaneous summer showers, hurricanes, fall color displays, and then the best: snow.

We were looking forward to the snow, as most of my children had never seen it, but our neighbors warned us that it didn't really snow that much around here anymore—something to do with temperature changes as the Washington metropolitan area kept spreading out to places like the rural community in which we were now planted.

So my children prayed for snow.

And, did it ever snow! Like the Christmas song written by Christina Rosetti, "In the Bleak Midwinter."

> *Snow had fallen,*
> *snow on snow,*
> *snow on snow on snow.*

In the rural area where we live, snow plows hadn't even cleared the road before the next snow began. Records were broken by the snow that fell our first Virginia winter together—including the heaviest snow ever for a rare White Christmas, and 30 inches in late February.

For the children in the area, it was like a movable feast—they'd go from one house to another—sledding at this one, hot chocolate at another, a movie here, a bonfire there. What a wonderful life it was! Every night I'd surf the Internet to our favorite weather page, with 9-year-old Madeleine and 10-year-old Jonny eagerly looking over my shoulder for the forecast. If snow was on its way, Jonny would point to the snow icon and clap his hands gleefully. Madeleine would run through the house announcing it like a town crier—thus earning her nickname, The Weathergirl. The next morning, if snow lay on the ground, we'd hit the School's Out web site to see if school had been canceled, which happened with alarming frequency—more than any local old-timers could remember.

It got so bad, at one point after four consecutive days of no school, a neighbor E-mailed me to say, "All right, already, I think the Curtises need to stop praying for snow or winter will never end."

Well, the winter did end. Most people heaved a sigh of relief after a rough winter of shoveling snow, keeping generators going, and trying to find parking spaces in lots with mountains of snow so high and so wide there was little room left for cars. We even spotted dump trucks by the highways being loaded with snow to carry off because it wasn't melting fast enough.

Our family, having enjoyed a four-month ecstatic experience, was somewhat sad, but our souls stood slightly ajar for the next one. And behold, it came as we experienced our first real spring, when everything went from gray to lush green and our neighbors' houses were once again hidden. Keep in mind California's very different meteorological year—two seasons, rain/no rain—plus not many deciduous trees. Not many leaves falling in the fall, not many to come back suddenly and splendidly in the spring.

And then, as if God hadn't blessed our family enough with ecstatic experience, He provided me with this personal exclamation point.

I was helping Madeleine find some information for a science report one day when we came across a web site with the weather icons. Jonny, who was standing at my desk looking on, pointed excitedly to the snow icon, and began jumping up and down with joy, remembering the snow. Clasping his hands together in a pleading way, he sang, "Pease, oh, Mommy, pease, can we get dat one?"—in the same way he points to cool things in toy catalogues and asks for them.

By now it was summer, but Jonny's abstract thinking skills hadn't grasped that some things just are not possible, and even though I said snow wouldn't come for a long time, he kept clasping his hands and pleading, "Pease, Mommy, pease?"

And then it hit me: my son thought I was responsible for the weather! Having seen me order things on the Internet—much more convenient for a megamom than a mall—he'd thought when we were checking the weather reports that winter that I was ordering the snow!

It doesn't get much better than that—when God can send you a greeting better than any Hallmark card through your children. Jonny's faith in his earthly mother—even though misguided —reminded me how OK it is to trust like a child in my Heavenly Father. And Jonny's jumping up and down for joy reminded me how ecstatic my experience is when my faith is utter and complete.

Over the 16 years since I became a believer, I may have matured in applying God's Word to daily living, but in one area I've never grown up. Forget the big theological debates. They're just a distraction from the jumping up and down for joy that's ours when we keep it sweet and simple.

And if my word's not enough, just remember Jesus', "I tell you the truth, unless you change and become like little children, you will never enter the kingdom of heaven" (Matt. 18:3).

Thought of this way, living with children is a privilege. Indeed, Jesus goes on to say, "Whoever welcomes a little child like this in my name welcomes me" (v. 5).

A privilege, but still a mighty challenge. I suppose that's why so many people express amazement that anyone would choose to have a large family or, in our case, simply leave our family size to God.[8] Sometimes the amazement is respectful, but sometimes it hurts, as when people say things like, "I don't know how you do it. My two are enough to drive me crazy."

It's embarrassing to hear another mother say this in front of her children—and mine. I want to grab her hand and say, "Stop!

Think! That's not the way it's supposed to be! These children are our treasures!"

Ps. 127 says:

> Sons [and daughters, I might add] are a heritage from the
> LORD,
>   children a reward from him.
> Like arrows in the hands of a warrior
>   are sons born in one's youth.
> Blessed is the man
>   whose quiver is full of them (vv. 3-5).

Sometimes in the daily grind, I lose sight of the fact that motherhood is not something God has burdened me with, but something He has blessed me with. I'm just like other mothers, really. Sometimes I wake up already tired, and the day ahead makes me wonder if the cynics I meet are really right and I really am a nutcase.

When I need a little extra oooomph, I wake up my kids with a little extra entertainment from Mom—sung to the tune of the Disneyland ride Pirates of the Caribbean:

> *Yo ho, yo ho, a mommy's life for me.*
> *We get up at dawn and put the pot on,*
> *Wake up, me 'earties, yo ho.*
> *We wake up the kiddles and fix 'em their vittles,*
> *Wake up, me 'earties, yo ho.*
> *Yo ho, yo ho, a mommy's life for me.*
> *Some think we're insane, but who can complain?*
> *Wake up, me 'earties, yo ho.*
> *Much work is in store, but blessings galore,*
> *Wake up, me 'earties, yo ho.*
> *Yo ho, yo ho, a mommy's life for me!*

And so I've surrendered to this mommy's life. But not everyone who asks how or why in the world I have will understand the concept of surrender. So I simplify and focus on the most self-

Sometimes in the daily grind, I lose sight of the fact that motherhood is not something God has burdened me with but something He has blessed me with.

centered reason I can think of: It's because I've found that in my feelings for my children, I've come as close as I can to God's feeling for me. Whether they've learned to turn a somersault, brought the hose in to water the dining room, scored a touchdown, warmed the bench all season, captured the lead in the play, started stammering again, made straight As, or been caught cheating, they've taught me this incredible lesson: how to love unconditionally.

Compared to God's love, of course, mine is just a vague reflection. But isn't it really the reason He put us here? Like the old Jewish proverb:

God couldn't be everywhere at once, so he made mothers.

Not-So-Perfect Motherhood

We'd counted down the days till *Les Miz*. I ordered the tickets well in advance—the first day they went on sale—and we splurged so we had great seats waiting. It was a weekday, and that year the older kids were in a Christian school, but the principal had agreed to excuse them early. After all, there were so many lessons to be learned from the story—lessons of grace and redemption—that it would more than make up for the lost school hours.

I'd also snagged a baby-sitter for the younger children for the six or seven hours we'd be gone, including travel to and from San Francisco, a good hour from where we lived then.

It was a gorgeous day, all the better to enjoy the sparkling view of the bay, ripples glimmering in sunlight, sailboats bobbing here and there. Then the breathtakingly beautiful Golden Gate Bridge, a marvel of engineering impossible to take for granted. And I guess no one does, because like a vain and aging movie star, it's in a constant state of makeover. In the 30 years I lived on either side, I never crossed it without seeing men at work. The bridge is red, not gold—Golden Gate is the name of the inlet it spans—and for some reason, the red repainting never, ever stops.

Zipping through the tollbooth, then up and down the giddy hills past pastel rows of flats, we landed in the theater district. We found a nearby parking lot, paid our fee in advance, and jostled our way through the crowds with kids tightly in tow—all while deciding which homeless people to give money to.[9]

I pulled the seven tickets from my bag and showed them to the usher at the door, who pointed us past the lush carpets and dazzling chandeliers to the flight of stairs leading to the balcony.

There another usher studied our tickets, then handed them back, telling us how many rows down we'd find our seats.

Our seats were where he said they'd be. But somehow they weren't awaiting us. Other people were sitting in them. I looked at the tickets again, double-checking the numbers.

"Excuse me, I think you've taken our seats," I said to the closest inhabitant, and showed her my handful of tickets.

"Oh, I'm sorry. Let's see," she said as she fumbled in her purse for her own tickets. Pulling them out, she examined them and then the seat markers before announcing, "No, our tickets are for these seats."

She was right. We both had sets of tickets for the same exact seats. Tripp went to get an usher, who compared the tickets and appeared as confounded as we were. The pressure was mounting as the orchestra was warming up, and the lights flickered to warn that in a few minutes the curtain would rise. And then the usher took another look—and saw that our tickets . . . were for the next day.

Gulp.

It was my mistake, no doubt about it. As in most families, Mom is the social coordinator, events facilitator, activity director, personal planner, calendar keeper, and all-around cheerleader for the family. I'd ordered the tickets, I'd push-pinned them on the bulletin board when they arrived, and I'd dutifully entered Les Miz on our calendar. Only one thing went wrong: I'd written it on the wrong day.

And so we'd wrangled permission to leave school early, gotten all gussied up, paid the baby-sitter, gas, toll, and parking—not to mention Tripp taking off work—all so we could do it again the next day.

Needless to say, the next day was anticlimactic. Still—as I pointed out repeatedly in a glass-half-full kind of way—at least we'd been a day early and not a day late.

It doesn't matter. I'll never live this one down. It persists in our family lore as "The Wrong Date." I know at my funeral, one of my kids—who I hope will be very, very old by then—will jab another with his cane and say, "Remember the day Mom got us to *Les Miz* on the wrong day?" and they will laugh so hard they'll cry.

OK, so no one's perfect. And I didn't have to be a mother to make a mistake like that. But it sure helps. Especially when you've got a lot of children.

Think about it. Unless you, dear reader, have 12 kids or more, I undoubtedly make many more mistakes than you do. It stands to reason: the more children a mother has, the more opportunities she has to make mistakes. An insurance company would understand. Just as they charge more to insure young male drivers because they have more accidents, if they wrote policies for parenting they'd have to charge more to cover the risks inherent in being a megamom.

If only they could! If only as they cover body work on a damaged vehicle they could bang out the dings and dents in my reputation when I do something out of the ordinary or, as happens more often, don't remember just to do the ordinary.

I'll never forget the first time we forgot a child. It was Sunday morning—eight kids then as I remember—and we were scurrying to get to church on time. When you're a big family and you attend a crowded church, you must arrive early if you all want to sit together. Tripp and I had a fallback when things were rushed: one of us would leave with whatever kids were ready and save seats for the stragglers who came later. Sometimes though, even the first shift couldn't make it in time to find 10 seats.

That's what happened this particular Sunday. Arriving later, and seeing Tripp and his group of kids were squeezed in with no room to spare, I settled my group in the only spot available—on the other side of the church. We sang, prayed, listened to readings. Then all of a sudden I got a creepy feeling.

I stared across the church at the side of Tripp's head, trying to generate a laser beam that would make him turn and look at me. Finally he did.

"Where's Zach?" I mouthed, exaggerating with my lips so he could read them.

I could see him counting heads. Then making a dash for the door. Finally he came and crouched beside my folding chair to let me know eight-year-old Zach was home alone, reading. I was surprised, but not surprised. So typical of our budding genius—to wrap himself in a book and let the world spin on without him.

From that moment on, I completely understood how the little guy in *Home Alone* got left alone. And unfortunately, I can't say it was the last time something like that happened. As our family grew and some of the teens had other plans, more often than not we'd end up taking two or even three vehicles to church. No matter how careful I was never to leave someone home alone again, in the flurry of stuffing everyone into car seats and seatbelts after church, once in a while someone got left at church. Then we'd get a call and have to drive back, completely embarrassed at our less-than-perfect parenting once again waving like a banner in the breeze for all to see.

I've had the experience of why-did-you-have-so-many-kids-if-you-couldn't-keep-track-of-them neighbors bringing back wandering kids, as well as the unpleasant surprise of arriving at church to find my three-year-old barefoot in the backseat because I'd asked big brother to put him in and big brother hadn't noticed. Only one way to handle it—carry him into Sunday School and act like it's just a slight oversight—even though I've never ever seen a barefoot child in Sunday School before.

But it's not just my kids that bring out the less-than-perfect mother in me. For whether it comes to sending in something I've been asked to send in or remembering to bring home my own stuff—on either side of the equation, I've lost track of bottles, diapers, wipes, lunches, juice boxes, milk money. You name it, I've forgotten it.

I've had months when the emergency room has been like a second home. I've had the fire engines at my house to remove Madeleine's six-month-old finger from the teensy hole of a bell where she'd gotten it stuck, also to turn off the fireplace gas when I turned it on with no results and then couldn't remember which way was off and which was on.

I've gone to potlucks empty-handed because I didn't have time to make or even buy anything but was so desperate for adult conversation I'd go and risk judgment. I've put my own houseplants on suicide watch. I've put writing before housework. I've gone days sometimes without sweeping my kitchen floor, shamelessly rationalizing, "What's the use? It'll be dirty in an hour anyway."

But that's not the worst. The worst is when I'm asked to write on a parenting topic, and just when I'm in the midst of gathering the most profound insights and serving them up to help someone else do a better job mothering, I start doing worse. Ask me to write about cultivating a good work ethic in kids, and all of a sudden my own kids are balking, lazy slobs. Ask me to write about encouraging words, and all of a sudden my family sounds like the Osbornes. Ask me to write about patience, and I'm guaranteed to lose my temper with my kids.

There, now that that's off my chest I feel better. I feel better because you need to know that we are in the same boat, you and I. I may have been doing this mothering thing longer—and so have gleaned some wisdom to share—but like you, I'm still learning how to be a better mom one day at a time. I'm still changing diapers, cleaning up messes, trying to get several sets of teeth brushed every night before collapsing completely.

The constant reminders of my imperfection keep me humble —even as I'm writing—and challenge me to practice what I preach.

They also help me understand how hard it is for mothers today. Each of us is trying so hard to be perfect. We find ourselves pressured from forces without and within, always feeling we can't keep up, we've fallen short, we'll never be as good as this one or that one. We feel—with or without any real basis—judged by others. And surely, we're constantly judging ourselves and our performance as mothers.

Motherhood has its difficult moments, and some stages are worse than others. I'm constantly telling mothers of toddlers that they're in the most demanding years (though now that I've raised more teenagers, I'm thinking I maybe should change my tune). In this day and age, when extended families are few and far between, mothers of young children too often struggle with feelings of loneliness and isolation. Mothers of Preschoolers (MOPS) was founded by just such a mother and has helped thousands of mothers feel more connected, less alone.[10]

But the striving for perfection can lead us into more serious sad places. It makes us competitive and inauthentic, so that we can't be honest about who we are or what is going on in our lives —especially with other mothers, the very ones who could look into our eyes and say, "Yes, I know how you feel. I feel that way too."

One young homeschooling mother of six tells me that the use of antidepressants among young Christian moms must be epidemic, if her local observation is true at large. I can't back this with research, because to my knowledge, doctors and pharmacists don't keep records of patients' religion.

Still, it wouldn't surprise me. American mothers—Christian or not—face unprecedented pressure to be perfect. Not just perfect wives and mothers, perfect cooks and housekeepers, but also perfect in appearance and personality. And if all the worldly pressure weren't enough, to top it all off, Christian women face the added burden of having to be constantly filled with joy!

OK, let's start with the worldly: movie stars arranging to give birth at seven months, to have their babies by Caesarian, and to have a personal trainer at their house the next day to help them immediately shed any signs that they've entered the realm of motherhood. And how about the anchorettes on the nightly news with the most perfectly tucked, sculpted, and botoxed faces money can buy? These produce cultural images of womanhood that are just impossible for most women to live up to.

But why should they have to? In other eras, other cultures, the normal thing would be for mothers to look like mothers. Take a tour through *National Geographic* to find an Italian mama sweating over the stove or a Mexican madre with rolled-up sleeves pounding tortillas or an African mother carrying a fish home on her head, proud of her catch and untroubled by breasts sagging from years of nursing the next generation. You don't see mothers in other countries looking like their kids' big sister.

The push for mothers to be glamorous has been a serious setback for American moms, just another impossible yardstick to measure ourselves against. I saw it clearly one afternoon while ironing (yes, ironing!) when I turned on the TV to see what was offered for moms to watch while their kids are in school. There, between the soaps and the talk shows, the ads for diapers and detergents, was a pair of back-to-back commercials that said it all: Victoria's Secret and Zoloft. The Victoria's Secret minute, backed by pounding runway music and bordering on soft porn, held out the image of a femme fatale in sexy bikini and bra—but held it out to whom? The audience for that noon-to-three TV slot is strictly housewives, so the message is clear that in addition to having babies and raising them, to keeping our homes a haven for our families, we are also supposed to be buying sexy underwear and practicing provocative poses.

No wonder we have postpartum depression.

The Zoloft commercial made it clear that women could erase any unwanted negative feelings with just a little pill.

Was this a setup—the Zoloft ad following on the heels of Victoria's Secret? I mean, it just seems too perfect in terms of sales potential to have been unplanned. Think about it: a young, overtired mother with a toddler or two or three might feel so depressed at the impossibility of measuring up to the Victoria's Secret ideal, she might opt for something more doable—like asking her doctor for a prescription to take away the depression caused by a gnawing sense of inferiority caused by all the TV images of women she can't live up to.

All around us, everyone's telling us what we should look like, act like, be like—how we should feed our families, decorate our houses, grow our gardens. TV shows galore, plus a swarm of women's magazines filled with makeovers, cosmetic and hair tips, not to mention an overabundance of articles on how to be a monogamous nymphomaniac. And, oh, in case you're too tired to even think about sex, not to worry—there are pills you can buy to fix that.

We're bombarded by cultural images of womanhood that are just impossible for most of us to live up to.

It makes me wonder how biblical couples managed to keep their marriages together. I guess they were just too busy dragging water from the well and feeding the camels to think about how to pluck the perfect eyebrow. What would Mary and Joseph have made of the concept of date nights or the checkout rack women's magazines' ever more graphic bedroom techniques?

And why do Christian marriage-improvement courses echo the same sentiments, only with Christian gloss? Where did we ever get the notion that we were supposed to work so hard at making marriage fun? Or even that marriage is supposed to be fun? And how does this all fit in with God's plan for marriage?

God established families for the purpose of partnering with Him in the raising of His children and of passing down from one generation to the next the knowledge and love and worship of Him. Everything we do to improve in this area is definitely worthwhile. The rest is just a bunch of distractions.

Hold on to that thought next time you start to feel you're falling short—not as thin, not as pretty, not as accomplished, not as sexy, not as energetic as this or that other woman you know. When you look around at school or church and see all the mothers who look perfect, just know that underneath, no matter how they appear, they feel the same way too.

In fact, I've come to the conclusion—based just on my own random observations—that the more together a mother looks, the more anxiety-ridden she really is.

One example: A few years ago I met a young mother of four young year-and-a-half-apart children. She had a beautiful home and loving husband and lots of friends. But she was miserable because she felt she was out of shape (having four children in six years has a way of doing that, doesn't it?). She found her salvation in swearing off more babies, losing a lot more weight than she needed to, and exercising till she looked like a budding junior bodybuilder.

I guess she looked great—though not at all like the comfortable mommy her kids once knew. And I had to wonder if she felt as great as she looked when one day as we watched our kids in a school performance, she nudged me and pointed, whispering, "Do you think she's skinnier than me? She says she is, but I don't think so" about another mother who'd also been very obviously on a self-improvement campaign—running every morning, new haircut and color, revitalized wardrobe.

You've got to admit, we women can be pretty strange. But as

revealing as this mother's question was about the insecurities that drove her, my guess is that almost every woman has the same nagging voice inside telling her she's just not good enough. And while those moms working on the physical can grab onto something concrete—their bottoms or their tummies—and work to make them better and see specific results, others carry around a big mess of vague doubts and anxiety based on something inside they just can't seem to put their fingers on. When it's not something you can see, it can be so much harder to figure out what exactly needs to be improved, much less how to improve it. And so, women become depressed or obsessed.

Like one neighbor of mine reputed to be obsessed with cleanliness—unhealthily so. How true the rumors were I learned when I saw her in the grocery store pulling out four or five boxes of cereal and reaching behind to get the one farthest into the shelf. She laughed nervously when she saw me and explained she liked to "just make sure." Make sure of what, I had to wonder. What worries was she running from?

We need to stop running from our worries and start running toward God. He's the only one we can trust to accept us as we are—even when we can barely accept ourselves. He won't push us aside to reach for the more perfect and spotless specimen behind.

Think of Jesus and those He gravitated toward—imperfect people all, His favorites. He had time to eat with the despised tax collectors and prostitutes. He had time for men He knew would let Him down. He did not have time for those who thought they were perfect—and tried hard to make others think so as well—like the Pharisees, whom He rebuked again and again, most harshly in Matthew 23. When the Pharisees asked His disciples, "Why does your teacher eat with tax collectors and 'sinners'?" Jesus himself answered, "It is not the healthy who need a doctor, but the sick" (Matt. 9:11-12).

So it's OK not to be perfect. Jesus said so. But is it OK to rest there? Is it OK to think that because God accepts us in our imperfection it's OK to stay that way forever? I've been in churches like that—churches where people who'd been stung by the legalism and self-righteousness of modern-day Pharisees completely rejected the idea of character improvement, tipping the scale a little too far on the side of grace.

Legalism is ugly, no doubt about it. But the sloppy agape of believers who focus exclusively on grace isn't a pretty sight either. Beauty is to be found in the balance of the two. And it's no less true in a mother's life—we need to lovingly accept ourselves as God accepts us, and we need to lovingly do our best to do better.

God is the only One we can trust to accept us as we are—even when we can barely accept ourselves.

The years I've spent with God have shown me that God is always lovingly nudging me to do better—much as I encourage my own children. Just because we've arrived at motherhood and are now teachers doesn't mean we're not still learning ourselves, after all. It reminds me of a medieval etching I once saw, with people ascending up to heaven—level by level—getting closer to God. Except for the bottom level, where people can only reach up, at the other levels individuals reach one hand up to be pulled upward by the one above them, while still reaching back to help those at the level below. Mother Teresa, one of my personal heroes, was a modern-day personification of that image—reaching down to help so many people while reaching up to become closer to God. Her writings reveal a soul eager to learn, even as she shares the things God had already taught her. Reading her, I feel as the lepers in her care must have felt as she gently soothed their wounds, never patronizing or puffed-up.

Some people are afraid to learn more about who they are, as though someone once upon a time convinced them there was something too hideous for words deep inside. But that's not how it is at all. God wants us first to see the truth about ourselves, and then He wants to set us free. He wants to set us free by showing us that we can—with His help—do better.

It's natural to feel regret after a mistake, but there's a big difference between the regret that comes when Satan, the father of lies, rubs it in, and when God, the Father of truth, confronts you because He wants to empower you to do better. You can count on God to lovingly reveal the things He wants you to fix—like He showed me how I needed to be a better mother. But you will be able to tell it's Him by the way He treats you—like a child who needs an encouraging hug rather than a good spanking.

My general rule of thumb: When Satan hounds you about your weaknesses, you feel tired, depressed, and full of despair. When God confronts you, you feel remorse, quickly followed by the desire to change and hope for the future.

But if our minds are cluttered with self-doubt and superficial worries, we might not hear the still small voice.

What if there were no distractions? What if we could turn off all the other input and only hear from God the ways He would like to see us improve? What kind of things might we hear? What kind of women might we become?

I don't want to miss a moment, not a single one. The farther I go on my journey, the more I see how far from perfect I am. Like Jean Valjean, the hero of *Les Miserables*, I'm a product of grace and redemption. But like the Golden Gate Bridge, it seems I will always be a work in progress.

Does that sound exhausting? It's really not at all. Jesus promised us: "Come to me, all you who are weary and burdened, and I will give you rest. Take my yoke upon you and learn from me, for I am gentle and humble in heart, and you will find rest for your souls. For my yoke is easy and my burden is light" (Matt. 11:28-30).

Let's face it, as mothers we're reminded several times a day at least that we will never be perfect. But our stress level can stay under control as long as we're conscious of that easy yoke and our perfect Partner.

I teach my kids that mistakes are valuable—they give us opportunities to learn and to do better. Sometimes we have to remember to apply to our lives the things we teach our children. The fact is, I've never gotten us someplace on the wrong day again. But there've been a multitude of other mistakes and "learning opportunities."

When I'm tempted to take it all—and myself—too seriously, I call to mind something my kids say to me now and then. They picked it up from *Driving Miss Daisy*, a great film on race and reconciliation that won an Academy Award back in the days when uplifting films won Academy Awards. In it Dan Ackroyd plays Jessica Tandy's grown-up son, and he has a standard refrain to her foibles and follies—said in a deep southern drawl, which my kids imitate perfectly when they say it to me:

"You're a doodle, Momma!"

Somehow, that puts it all in perspective.

❧ 6 ❧

Serving from the Heart

Once upon a time—when we lived where houses were within walking distance—my four sons had paper routes. Because Tripp and I had built a business together, we very much wanted to cultivate our kids' entrepreneurial spirit, and so we were grateful for the opportunity to help them learn about keeping commitments, working for wages, and handling accounts.

We were also grateful they'd have a way to earn money other than the rat-raising business, in which they fattened up the mamas and kept the papas from eating their own offspring until the babies were big enough to be sold to pet stores. There were always plenty of babies—and money to be made—but the downside to this thriving enterprise was the mess of cedar shavings that littered the area around the cages without ever really conquering the pungent odor of rats. And then there was the loss of a few along the way, who'd somehow managed to slip out and were probably kicking up their heels at the freedom they'd found in our attic.

No question about it, the newspaper route seemed less of a struggle—especially since it was only an afternoon weekly.

On Wednesdays, after a morning of homeschool, the boys and I kept a lookout on the driveway for the big bundles of papers. Between them, the boys had about 200 subscribers. Upon the arrival of the papers, we dragged them into the garage where we folded them in thirds, slid a rubber band around (on rainy days a plastic bag), and loaded them into their carrier bags.

I'd drop the boys off one by one at their start points, then pick them up at the end of their routes. I'll never forget the dedication and determination on the face of eight-year-old Zach, staggering beneath the weight of his bag. His route covered two long, flat blocks of mostly retired people who anxiously awaited their Wednesday paper, some even walking down their sidewalks to meet him before he could get to their doors.

No doubt in his mind that a paper route was a worthy endeavor! When I picked him up, no matter how exhausted, he glowed.

Things like this brought out the glow in me as well. Over my years of mothering, I've found no matter what I set out to teach my kids or how, God never fails to send a few lessons my way too.

One has to admire our Father's efficiency.

On the other side of delivering papers was collecting the money. Crucial, because each boy was billed for all the papers dropped on our driveway that month. To break even, each needed to collect from at least two-thirds of his customers. So collecting involved lessons in record-keeping, courtesy, and—most of all—perseverance.

Summer collections were cinchy, but it always took a little extra oomph to get out the door on winter nights, when dark fell early and cold whipped through the hills of suburban California like a most unpopular party crasher.

On one such night, I packed the boys in the van after dinner and we headed out to round up money together. Each boy was loaded with change in his pocket, pen and clipboard in hand.

We decided to tackle 10-year-old Ben's route, with its roller-coaster hills, first. Heater blasting, we wound our way to the first address. I stopped the car, shut off the ignition, and turned to shoo my third son out the door.

The front porch light gleamed in the dark, assuring us Ben would not stumble. But it also illuminated something special for me—a radiant smile spreading over my son's face.

"The nicest people in the world," Ben said, before he stepped out into the cold. With the engine off, his brothers and I blew on our hands to keep them warm. Ben came back with dimples flashing.

We drove up four doors to Ben's next customer. As I turned off the engine, Ben beamed again.

"The nicest people in the world!" he said.

"I thought the first house was the nicest people in the world," I said.

"Yeah, but these people are too," Ben said, sincere as sunshine. Another big smile, another big tip.

We replayed this scene again and again. Soon Ben's brothers and I forgot the cold, warmed by Ben's infectious love of the people he served. Soon we were all chanting, "The nicest people in the world," in front of each customer's house.

Back home, snuggled in a warm bed and waiting for sleep, I flashed back on my memories of Ben's action-packed life—a mother's way of counting sheep, only more fun.

"He has dimples!" My first words when he was born—and often the first thing people notice about Ben. Dimples, as though God marked him especially for merriment. Ben was a funny baby, who laughed at the drop of a hat and could barely stop once started.

But, boy, was he ever serious about work. As soon as he could walk he found certain jobs that needed doing—like turning off the dishwasher. The minute anyone closed the dishwasher door and pushed the start button, he'd toddle over full of purpose and turn it off. We'd wait until he toddled off to the next room to turn it on again, but sure enough, the minute he heard the swish of water he'd be back to do his duty. Six or seven times he'd go through the same routine before someone would just not turn it back on, but wait for him to go outside or take a nap. Six or seven times with the same good-natured determination and not a flicker of frustration.

It was his job and he enjoyed it.

Another Ben job was shoveling the ashes from the kitchen fireplace and carrying them to the living room fireplace, only spilling half of them along the way.

And don't forget the time he brought in the garden hose to water the carpet. Let's face it, the boy had always had a thing about enjoying his work.

Of course, he and his brothers had always seen their parents enjoying their work. Tripp and I are both oldest children and hence work-oriented, Type A personality overachievers.[11] When we married, Tripp was working for a tug and barge company on the bay, a job that brought him an enormous sense of gratification—feeling like a big hero as he'd dash out for an emergency oil spill cleanup at three in the morning—and brought me an enormous amount of frustration for the same type reason.

Imagine! The man seemed to like his work more than staying home with me! Now I wonder what in the world I was thinking, realizing some women would be grateful for a man who loved to work.

Anyway, I made Tripp's life miserable until he quit. You can imagine how miserable that had to be when I place this in context: we had two daughters and a son on the way, lived in a rented house, and had a single small car between us. No savings, of course.

Tripp's heart was at sea—and he hoped to return there—but in order to put food on the table, he fell back to an old skill—taking care of people's trees. You know, those men you see with saddles and ropes strapped into the tree as they prune. After high school Tripp had worked for a tree service. He still had his saw and saddle. And since he'd grown up in Marin County, where we lived, he knew lots of people with lots of trees.

He'd go out with his chainsaw and fill up the trunk of our car with branches to take to the dump. It wasn't something he wanted to do the rest of his life—but as days turned into weeks and weeks turned into months—and still no job on the bay, the tree business seemed to take on a life of its own. Tripp hired an assistant with a pickup truck so he could pack more for the dump. Finally he saved enough to buy his own truck—then his first chipper, which really made him more efficient. Then he needed more employees, insurance, payroll tax withholdings, and on and on.

Somewhere in that process, Tripp realized that the work God had planned for him was not the work he'd thought he wanted. That's easy for me to put into words, but it was a crisis for Tripp to live through. He vividly remembers his moment of surrender:

As I worked on the trees each day, I dreamed of the sea. Especially as the summer began to simmer, I began to simmer too. Our baby was due next month, and while Barbara was feeling content that I was home every night, I was feeling resentful and full of despair.

One day my assistant called in sick. That left me with an achy arm and a big job to do alone. I was working on the street where I grew up, in Mr. Sanor's backyard, trimming back a high and unruly hedge. The work was not going well because the lever that pulled the blade of my pole pruner shut kept sticking. I was getting hotter, sweatier, dirtier, and crankier by the minute. Things just weren't going my way, not only on this job but with my whole life. As my frustration mounted, I found myself arguing with God: I just don't understand! Why can't I get back to the sea? Am I supposed to be stuck in these trees for the rest of my life?

Suddenly, as though I had reached the eye of the hurricane, my whirlwind of emotions came to rest. I was filled with peace. Perhaps it was because I asked a direct question that I heard an answer. Suddenly I was filled with assurance and a sense of purpose. Serving others and taking care of creation was to be my calling. What better way to be there for my wife and children, as well as to contribute to my community!

I remember that day because for the first time, Tripp came home at peace, ready to embrace his calling. The next week, he was working for an Irish lady who brought him out a cup of coffee and said in a thick brogue, "You know, they really ought to call you Mr. Trees." When Tripp told me, I knew that was our company's name.

We made business cards and flyers. And for years I'd hike up and down the hills of Marin through the nicest neighborhoods with Josh in a baby carrier on my back—then Matt in a baby carrier and Josh in a stroller, then Ben in a baby carrier . . . well, you get the picture. For years—until we were expecting No. 6, Zach—I answered the phone, scheduled appointments, helped Tripp make decisions, and designed Mr. Trees advertising.

By the time Zach was born, we'd moved the office out of our house and hired someone to do my work. Now we owned the biggest (25 employees, a fleet of trucks, and what seemed like an endless supply of dangerous tools and machines) and the most highly rated tree company in Marin.

A real Local-Boy-Makes-Good story, and one that proves to me that in this country you really can accomplish anything if you work hard enough. I remember one Memorial Day, Tripp was working and so was I as we struggled to keep growing our business and finding work for our employees. Sweaty and tired, I was pushing the baby stroller up yet another hill, delivering flyers. The smell of barbecues hung in the air, as well as laughter from people having fun in their pools. "Someday we'll be able to take a day off and play in our own pool," I thought. It was only a few years before we did have a house, a pool, and even once in a while, some time to play.

OK, so this is my story, not Tripp's—but for those years when God called Tripp to start a tree business, He called me to help him launch it. It was difficult sometimes working together and being reminded of each other's faults. After all, Tripp didn't come home to hear, "How was work today, honey?" but rather, "You forgot to call Mrs. So-and-So like you promised." Likewise, he had to deal with my mistakes in addresses, dates, directions. But it was exciting working together to build something useful and good. And it was possible for me to have the best of both worlds —working at the Mr. Trees desk at home while the kids napped or even nursing a baby.

When the time came to move on because the business and our family had each become too big to share me, it felt fine to give it up. And it wasn't long before homeschooling became my next calling.

But a child's education begins long before we send him or her off to school or before we sit down to teach him or her lessons. And for my own children, part of their early education was seeing Mom and Dad at work, hearing us on the phone with customers, discussing employee problems, dealing with equipment break-downs, paying bills. And most exciting, Daddy up in the trees. For them, work wasn't a compartmentalized part of your life but integrated into the family.

Even today as I write, my work is integrated into the family life. Although now I send my children off to school each morning (one of the great advantages of moving from California to Virginia was to have a school system I could trust with my children— though I monitor it closely) and have three hours to write in peace, I originally began writing while homeschooling. This meant I had to learn to write in a way different from most writers. I couldn't afford wasted time. I had to be able to tune in and focus fast, to write a sentence or a paragraph or a page—whatever I had time for before being interrupted.

My office has two doors—one opening into the playroom. There is also a loveseat beside my desk as well as toys and books for the kids. Sometimes my whole family is in my office as I write, and I've learned to switch my attention back and forth.

All this—Tripp's story, my story—is by way of saying that I

believe deep down inside that we can do whatever God calls us to do, regardless of our circumstances. God doesn't call the equipped, He equips the called.

And because of our callings, my children have grown up with parents who love to work. So they've taken on their little enterprises—the rats and the newspapers—with enthusiasm. After the newspapers came Brothers Firewood, where they partnered to split and deliver firewood and learned that if you're not careful and bang into a mailbox you can lose all your profit replacing it. And there were part-time jobs in summer and after school—scooping ice cream, delivering packages, refinishing floors.

Through it all, and through the years of household chores and mowing lawns and raking leaves, I've tried to teach my children that we have no choice about working, but we do have a choice about how to respond. We can hate work and try our best to avoid it or give only the bare minimum. Or we can embrace our work, do more than is expected of us, and choose to enjoy the time we spend.

When my kids were little, I made the most of Disney's *Snow White* and all it has to teach about work. The dwarves love to go off to their work in the mines, singing

> "We work, work, work, work, work, work, work work,
> Work the whole day through.
> We dig, dig, dig, dig, dig, dig, dig
> That's what we like to do."

The dwarves love digging, but they hate housework. Snow White teaches them to love that, too, with the wonderful work song "Just Whistle While You Work." And her own love of working makes cleaning the house a transcendent experience. I believe if I could model that same attitude consistently, I could communicate it to my kids and they would never have to carry the burden of hating housework.

Also dear to my heart, and something I've tried my best to

communicate to my children, is this idea: all work is noble and deserving of respect and God sees our work and is pleased by it as long as we do our best and maintain a good attitude.

We can do whatever God calls us to do, regardless of our circumstances.

I have a Mary Engelbreit card on my Inspiration Board (more about that later) that puts it this way: *To Be Happy, Don't Do Whatever You Like, Like Whatever You Do.* A happy housewife is dancing with her vacuum cleaner in one hand, a feather duster in the other, a rose like a tango dancer's in her teeth.

I've never liked it when people scorn some kinds of work, as when they say, "What do you want—to be flipping burgers for the rest of your life?" That's an insult to all those who do that kind of work. And I've met many who do it with cheerful attitudes and a lot of grace. And think about this: those kinds of jobs are great stepping-stones for people new to the workforce, as they learn things like punctuality and honesty and working under pressure. How wrong it is to put their work down!

I don't think God ranks our work at all. I don't think He values neurosurgeons more than janitors or airplane pilots more than parking lot attendants or U.S. senators over stay-at-home mommies. In fact, judging by what He has told us, those who do the lowliest and most unappreciated work probably find greater favor in God's sight. After all, God has great love for "the least of these." And no fewer than seven passages in three of the four Gospels remind us that the first shall be last—as in Matt. 20:26-28: "Instead, whoever wants to become great among you must be your servant, and whoever wants to be first must be your slave—just as the Son of Man did not come to be served, but to serve, and to give his life as a ransom for many."

Does that mean that someone in a high position or with a status-packed job can't find favor with God? Not at all. It all depends on attitude.

I think of Dr. Michael Harrison, the pediatric surgeon who operated several times on Jonny at the University of California at San Francisco, where he was taken immediately after he was born. UCSF is a teaching hospital, so patients are cared for by and family members deal with doctors in all stages of their education—from interns and residents to teaching physicians. In contrast to the often-swaggering, puffed-up-and-full-of-themselves students who attended Jonny, we found Dr. Harrison to be a refreshingly real and humble person who treated a teeny baby with Down syndrome as if he were a crown prince and his parents as if he had all the time in the world to set their minds at ease.

Only later did we learn he was a world-class physician who pioneered prenatal surgery and was written of in many magazines. To me, he is a living example of the way God intends us to pursue our calling—with humility and grace. I suspect that Dr. Harrison treats everyone as equals, and I'd like to think that he would never sneer at a burger-flipper.

But the fact is, we don't see that combination of high status and humility as often as we should. That may explain why Jesus told His disciples, "It is easier for a camel to go through the eye of a needle than for a rich man to enter the kingdom of God" (Matt. 19:24). He didn't say it was impossible, just that it was exceedingly difficult.

I mean, God needs all kinds of workers, so someone has to occupy the places our society holds in high regard. But they have to work extra hard not to let their worldly value go to their heads. My own work runs the gamut from cleaning messes up off the floor to writing for and teaching other mothers. Always in the forefront of my mind is that both are equally important in God's eyes, and that cleaning the messes may actually be more important because only God sees it.

You see, work is a love language—one of the five listed in Gary Chapman's *The Five Love Languages:* quality time, words of affirmation, gifts, acts of service, physical touch. But it's a love language only if the person working or serving has the right heart about what he or she does.

This is the key to understanding the whole Mary/Martha controversy—which for years, as a new believer, I found completely frustrating. You know the story: Jesus came to visit Mary and Martha. Mary sat listening at His feet.

But Martha was distracted by all the preparations that had to be made. She came to him and asked, "Lord, don't you care that my sister has left me to do all the work by myself? Tell her to help me!"

"Martha, Martha," the Lord answered, "you are worried and upset about many things, but only one thing is needed. Mary has chosen what is better, and it will not be taken away from her" *(Luke 10:40-42).*

Mommies should learn to determine if their child's "love language" is quality time, words of affirmation, gifts, acts of service, or physical touch.

For years, I was tormented with the familiar interpretation: Mary chose the highest path by setting her work aside to devote her attention to Jesus. I was tormented because I didn't identify with Mary at all—I mean, in those days if the Lord had come to my house, I know I'd have been in the kitchen making Him a meal. Service is my own love language—or had you already guessed?

So Jesus' rebuke of Martha seemed inappropriate and unnecessarily harsh. Jesus himself certainly used the love language of service, so why did it seem that He didn't understand Martha's heart at all?

Ah, but He did—and I believe it wasn't Martha's work but Martha's heart that was the problem.

Think about it: if Martha had been out in the kitchen preparing food for Jesus with her heart and mind focused on Jesus, if she'd been dancing like Snow White or Mary Engelbreit's vacuum/tango housewife—filled to overflowing with joy for the privilege of serving Him, Jesus would have seen that it was good and not rebuked her.

But Martha worked with bitterness and resentment, "distracted by all the preparations that had to be made." *Vine's Dictionary* translates "distracted" as "over-occupied." In other words, Martha was giving too much thought to her work and not enough to Jesus.

She was comparing and measuring and judging Mary to be less because she wasn't working as hard. Of course, all of us are subject to negative thoughts, but as someone has said, you have to treat them like unexpected guests—don't let them unpack their bags and keep them moving. Martha's problem was that she entertained the thoughts, worrying them like a dog with a bone. Then, when she was ready to explode, she came out and scolded our Lord like a fishwife, even ordering Him to make her sister work.

Just imagine!

Then picture how it might have been if Martha had read the *Love Language* book. Then she'd have simply shrugged off any mean thoughts by smiling and noting that while her love language was acts of service, Mary's was quality time.

And if she'd read *Lord, Please Meet Me in the Laundry Room*, she'd have remained serene—having learned that you can work and worship, work and pray, work and listen at His feet.

For those whose love language is service, who may have also struggled with the Mary/Martha thing, these words of Amy Carmichael will surely resonate: *One can give without loving, but one cannot love without giving.*

Ben, in his own childish way, had learned that lesson. Through serving them, he had fallen in love with the people on his paper route.

At about the same time, I was learning the same lesson—about my readers. I was learning that for the kind of writing I wanted to do and to reach the women I wanted to reach, it wasn't enough to just have something to say. I needed to fall in love with my readers so that all I said would be motivated by love and a sincere desire to empower mothers to find more joy each day in fulfilling their calling. I got a big bulletin board and filled it with pictures of mothers I knew with their families. As readers began picking up my first books and articles, they began to send me pictures too, so that now my board is almost covered (but there's always room for more!) with pictures of mommies.

I call it my Inspiration Board, and it hangs over my desk, so I can glance up from my computer now and then and breathe in the knowledge that I'm not just writing, but I'm writing for someone.

As mothers, we are already in love with the people we serve—only once in a while we get tired and forget. My prayer is that those moments of forgetfulness will become fewer and farther between as we continue to become more conformed to the image of Christ. My prayer is that when we forget, God will remind us—as He did me that night with Ben.

Ben's beautiful expression of love for those he served became a defining moment for our family. Though we folded and delivered our last newspaper many years ago, the lessons we learned stayed with us. Even now, "The Nicest People in the World" remains part of our family's idiom—a reminder of the gladness of heart when we forget ourselves and think more highly of those we serve.

One can give without loving, but one cannot love without giving.
. . . Amy Carmichael

It reminds me of Jesus, the truest Servant, who looked past sin and shame and treated those He came to serve as "The Nicest People in the World." Like those who answered Ben's knock on the door that night, like you and me, the people around Jesus were just ordinary people. They smelled like fish, quarreled among themselves, harbored political agendas, and eventually betrayed Him. Compared to the religious leaders, they looked like a sorry lot.

But when I think of Jesus kneeling before His disciples to wash their dirty feet, I don't see Him gritting His teeth to do the dirty work. I see a dazzling smile on His face—not serving because He had to but because He loved so much He couldn't help himself.

Matt. 25:40 says it all, "I tell you the truth, whatever you did for one of the least of these brothers of mine, you did for me."

O Lord, it's not about me, but all about You, after all. May we serve our families, our friends, our communities not because we have to, but because we, like You, are so infused with Your love that we just have to!

❦ 7 ❧

Just a Mommy

It was the kind of splendid September day when sending kids to school just feels wrong. Luckily, that year I was homeschooling and calling the shots. Plus we were living in California then, an hour from the Pacific Ocean. For all I knew, it could be the last day of summer, and we wouldn't want to miss that. So it was off to the beach with five children under eight—Josh, Matt, Ben, Zach, and Sophia.

Obviously, one of those easier-said-than-done kind of things.

But I was highly motivated—and so were the kids. Together, we cleaned up from breakfast, prepped the car, then gathered beach blankets, umbrella, towels, swimsuits, diapers, sunglasses, sand toys, first-aid kit, sunscreen, a cooler full of snacks and drinks—ay yi yi yi yi! Hello, motherhood—good-bye spontaneity.

I loaded the assorted car seats and strapped, snapped, and buckled five wiggling bodies into Big Blue, the 1989 Suburban we grew out of only a few years later. Back then, we'd never have dreamed that Suburbans would be trendy by the turn of the century. For us, it was the only vehicle with the right number of seats for our family.

Finally we were on the road, singing away with Raffi (back in the pre-Wiggles days) and counting down the miles to Heart's Desire.

Heart's Desire was a beach on Tomales Bay where I took the kids when Tripp wasn't there to make sure we didn't lose them to the crashing waves or undertow of the ocean. Heart's Desire tickled the kids' toes with just the teensiest ripples lapping at the shore. Josh could walk out a few hundred feet and still not be over his shoulders. It was kind of like a great big swimming pool—only with sand and occasional seasonal jellyfish.

With everyone else in school, the whole beach was ours. I staked out our territory close to the water, situated Sophia in her walker, hauled everything down from the car, and set up camp—ready to serve as personal valet, sunscreen slatherer, weather adviser, recreation director, swim instructor, lifeguard, EMT, food concessionaire, manners consultant, busboy, interpreter, peace negotiator, psychologist—not to mention lost and found.

Five hours later, I hauled everything back to the car, strapped, snapped, and buckled five sunscreen-and-sand-coated, no-longer-wiggly, warm, limp bodies back into Big Blue, and headed for home.

The sun through the window was soothing, and the car was full of contentment. It had been a wonderful day, and I was pleased with myself as a mother.

Then from the backseat I heard Zachary clear his throat and in his deadpan four-year-old Eeyore voice ask, "Mom, when are you going to get a job?"

"This is my job," I said, maybe just a little edgy.

But homeward bound, as the kids fell asleep one by one and I was left alone with my thoughts, I began to see the beauty of Zach's question: somehow—even though it could be hard work and even though I had my testy moments—my kids didn't think of motherhood as a job.

And I decided that was a good thing—because it's not really a job at all, but a calling. And callings just don't look like jobs, because they require more of a person than a job requires. Think of missionaries—for them it's not about the hours or money or status or rewards. They are just obedient to the call.

≈≈≈≈≈≈

I always wanted to be a mommy. Though in my wayward

years, I would stray from that call, putting myself and my own desires first, signs were woven into my girlhood that this was my dream. It wasn't programming or brainwashing, but something I now believe God planted deep in my heart.

Consider: With only the weakest link to my mother, who worked too hard to care, I grew up without an attractive role model. But I somehow had this strong love for and desire to protect babies and little children. At 10, I spent hours scouring old magazines for pictures of babies—pictures I'd cut out and taped to my otherwise-bare bedroom walls.

Remember how I shared that after becoming a believer, I was led to work on my self-honesty and willingness to change to become the mother God wanted me to be? Well, it wasn't long before I realized that even though I didn't have the background to be a good mother, from the beginning He'd called me. And finally—true to His promise to equip the called—my Heavenly Father equipped me.

Motherhood isn't a job—it's a calling. And a calling doesn't look like a job because it requires so much more of you.

It may seem selfish that shortly after Samantha was born I put her in day care and went back to college and then to Montessori school—and indeed, it was selfish. Selfish was the only way I knew how to behave in those days. *Alcoholics Anonymous*, the recovery bible that teaches survivors to be fearlessly honest, puts it this way: "Was he not a self-seeker even when kind?" So yes, my desire was to improve the condition of children, which seems noble enough till you notice that to realize my dream of helping children, I had to put my own daughter in day care.

That irony is not lost on me.

But the double irony is this: though I did go on to teach in schools ranging from poor inner-city Washington, D.C., to wealthy Marin suburbs, my Montessori training and what it taught me about children became most useful in a way I never dreamed of until I ended up having 12 of my own. And blessing on blessing, since then, God has given me the incredible privilege of sharing what I've learned through my own years of motherhood.

Which is how it comes about that we're having this discussion, you and I. And if I had my druthers, we'd be sipping tea or coffee together, and I could take your hands and give you this special blessing: *May God bless your motherhood as He has mine. May He give you the courage to see your mistakes and the assurance that He can use every one of them to His advantage. May He give you a vision of the glory of your motherhood, so that even while doing the lowliest tasks, you will not forget the privilege of your calling.*

I don't know how to explain how my mistakes became part of a plan, except as Martin Luther said, "For whoever believes, everything is beneficial and nothing is harmful. For those who do not believe, everything is harmful and nothing is beneficial."

I believe that even before I believed, when I was busy making mistake after mistake, God was in it with me for the long haul. That is not to say that He caused everything to happen the way it did—just that He walked with me through it all. We take it for granted that we can unfold a very large map and lay it out on the floor and easily see way beyond what is visible to us in these three dimensions. That's how I see God—as being able to see not only beyond the three-dimensional boundaries but way beyond the boundary of time.

We have freedom of choice. We have the freedom to make mistakes. But in His infinite mercy—which I feel so up-close and personally simply because I see my life not as about what I've done for myself or others or even Him, but about what He's done for me—God releases something better than we could have dreamed.

It's a miraculous process. I heartily agree with Anne Lamott: "It's not that I believe in miracles, I depend on them."

I depend on God to continue equipping me to fulfill this calling. At 55, I'm no spring chicken. Being an older mother has its rewards—the wisdom that comes from the things I've done right and the things I've done wrong, the mellowness, the patience—or is that just another name for exhaustion? Madeleine, my youngest birth child, is 10, but I also have three younger adopted sons with Down syndrome—two who are still in diapers (add me to your prayer list!).

It can be difficult staminawise. There are days I collapse at the end, thinking that most women my age are empty nesters who get their hair and nails done and have lives of their own. If they have their grandchildren over, they can rest for the next day or two. But my life tugs me here and there like the Energizer Bunny, until I actually do run out of juice, wondering, "Why me, Lord?"

Then I hear the answer clearly, "Why not you?" And I'm reminded that it's a simple day-to-day dependence on God to keep equipping me. It's not something He did before I became a mother—it's something He does every day.

What a privilege to be so dependent, so connected to Him. And no doubt about it, it's the connectedness to God that's key in realizing that being a mommy is a completely worthy—and unique—calling.

You don't hear many people saying that these days. Most girls grow up being indoctrinated with the idea that it's not enough to be a mommy. I say indoctrinated because I mean just that. I say indoctrinated because I think teaching girls that it's not enough to be a mommy goes against the natural tendencies observable in almost every little girl.

Even a radical feminist like me had to rethink my position

when I started having children. Especially upon having a string of four boys, who from the get-go were so different from the way Samantha and Jasmine had been. Sound effects were just a natural part of boy vocabulary. Physically, they took more risks. And No. 1 on their hit parade were guns, guns, guns—or whatever substitutes they could find since I had a weapons ban until Josh was four[12] (see note for what changed my mind).

Around that time, our family was blessed with a long-awaited girl, Sophia Rose. Yes, we dressed her in pink, but as the seventh child in a megafamily, she didn't learn by one-on-one input from Mom as much as from tagging after her older siblings. And since Samantha and Jasmine were much older and since we were homeschooling, that meant her real mentors were her four brothers.

It's the connectedness to God that's key in realizing that being a mommy is a completely worthy—and unique—calling.

Our house was filled with toy cars and trucks, Legos, plastic cowboys and army men, plus—following the Curtis version of the Second Amendment—assorted guns, knives, and swords. We also had a toy kitchen, which my boys had shown a little interest in—presumably because it had to do with food. I had bought my boys dolls thinking it would encourage them to be good daddies someday, but they rarely played with them and when they did usually created some elaborate hostage-taking and rescue situation.

As Sophia moved beyond rattles, we got her some girl-type stuff. Still, with boy toys outnumbering girl stuff four to one, and with four guys constantly engaged in boy pursuits, I never saw

Sophia pick up an airplane and go, "Vroom" or a gun and go, "Pow-pow."

She was always and ever 100 percent girl.

Like most girls, Sophia enjoyed nurturing and caring for her baby dolls, as well as creating her own simple soap operas with her dollhouse family. And since childhood play isn't about play at all but about building a foundation for our future work and relationships, I believe that almost all girls left to their own devices would choose marriage and motherhood over just a job. And history and tradition—among almost every culture—is on my side.

But I didn't care much for history and tradition back in the 1960s and 1970s, finding my bearings as a radical feminist in the Second Wave of Feminism—so-called because our intentions were to go further than the turn-of-the-century First Wave that had secured women's right to vote.

The Second Wave rolled more out of the antiwar movement than out of the First Wave of Feminism. Its founding mothers, one of which I prided myself to be, were political activists fed up with being called chicks and taken for granted by counterculture males who hogged the stage at rallies while we did the usual behind-the-scenes work. Our philosophies weren't based on the writings of original suffragettes (who had actually likened abortion to slavery) as much as on modern works like Betty Friedan's *The Feminine Mystique*, Simone de Beauvoir's *Second Sex*, which railed against the traditional role of women, which the authors claimed was inferior to men.

So in addition to sensible goals like equal education opportunities and equal pay for equal work and more books about girls (at that time, they were actually hard to come by), from its inception, the feminist movement was fighting for abortion and doing its best to get women out of the home and into the marketplace.

Now, 30 years later, I look back and see how wrong we were in our disdain for women who wanted to stay home and raise their children. Instead of addressing the real issue, which has to do with how much or how little value our society places on the family and the role of parents in shaping the next generation—instead of understanding that women were unhappy because their role as mothers needed more honor and affirmation—feminists simply pumped up the volume on the putdowns of motherhood.

And in a quarter of a century, what began as a fringe political movement became the prevailing thought in our culture, as women bought into the philosophy that they could have/should have a job and children too. By the time Samantha (born in 1969, a year before I became a feminist) and Jasmine (1975) graduated from high school, it was assumed among their friends that all of them would have careers. They went to college to prepare—some nurturing a secret hope of finding Mr. Right. Most still haven't.

Samantha said no to college and went to work, biding time until she and her high school sweetheart could afford to get married, which they did at 19. Together, they put her husband Kip through school, where he became a dot.com whiz. He's now the successful father of five—and since the birth of her first baby, Samantha's always been "just a mommy," though fitting in some at-home bookkeeping for Mr. Trees.

Jasmine didn't have a high school sweetheart, but she knew what she wanted—marriage and a family. Always eager to learn, but not in a school setting, she absolutely did not want to go to college. Our friends—even believers—urged us to make her go, with comments like, "How will she ever find a husband?" We looked around our church at all the young Christian women coming home with degrees and no husbands on the horizon— looking self-sufficient but a bit brittle—and we decided to back Jasmine's faith that if God had a husband for her, she didn't have to go far from home and spend thousands of dollars to find him. She was 21 when she met Nathan, a handsome 25-year-old former Army Ranger. A few months later, they were engaged, and in less than a year married. He's now a successful father of three—and Jasmine's "just a mommy."

Growing up in a household with a successful dad and their own "just a mommy" (who spent a few years helping from home with the family business and now writes when there is time), plus two "just a mommy" big sisters, my 20-year-old son, Josh, is looking for a wife who understands that, yes, it is enough to be "just a mommy."

It's not easy. Boomer mothers who grew up during feminism's heyday find it difficult to switch gears, especially if they were working mothers themselves.

But during the past decade a backlash has grown among younger women (yay!) against the feminist movement and the problems it has created for them and for our culture. For one thing, many are resentful of having grown up in day care or as latchkey kids or even with nannies. They're writing books about it,[14] and they're making their own life decisions to opt out of the I-can-have-it-all spinning-plates routine and simply stay home to raise their children. Many who never had their own "just a mommy" want to be one themselves.

We need to support these brave young women, not put down their goals as though they aren't as worthy as those of the college- or career-bound. Otherwise we send the message that a mother isn't equal to a dental hygienist or a social worker or an accountant. That motherhood alone doesn't offer fulfillment.

God has a plan for each of us. Parents need to simply tune in to what God wants for each of our children as individuals and support God's plan, even if it's different from what we expected. Parents who have predetermined agendas miss passing on to daughters and sons an important building block in our faith—the ability of each believer to hear the still small voice and to be ready to alter course at the slightest hint that He would have us do so.

As someone who's altered her course in radical ways, I can promise only that the rewards are worth the risk. God knows what He's doing—whether we do or not.

And I think God knew what He was doing when He created men and women with differences that would enable them to fulfill different, but complementary, roles, hinted at in Gen. 1:27:

> *So God created man in his own image,*
> *In the image of God he created him;*
> *male and female he created them.*

As a feminist, I scoffed at the idea of innate differences between men and women—other than the physical, of course. In the 1970s, prevailing thought held that who we were was completely determined by social conditioning. The reason boys were "masculine" was because we didn't coo at them as babies or give them dolls. And the reason girls grew up to be "just a mommy" was because their other talents were stifled.

Over the last few decades this kind of thinking oozed into every aspect of our culture and radically altered public schools. Ironic, because at the same time researchers were producing much evidence that our differences were indeed innate.

Their findings showed that even as infants, boys have higher levels of testosterone, which stimulates aggressive behavior, and lower levels of serotonin, which inhibits it. Researchers have found that infant boys cry more when unhappy while girls tend to comfort themselves by sucking their thumbs. Their conclusion: girls may be more able to control their emotions.

Newborn girls spend more time than newborn boys maintaining eye contact with adults. At four months, infant girls have better face recognition than boys. Conversely, infant boys are better able to track a blinking light across a TV monitor (a portent of adolescent video fixation?) and will gaze as intently at a blinking light as at a human face.

Yes, in addition to these innate differences (nature), there is also the tendency to treat boys like boys and girls like girls (nurture). But the innate differences are undeniably stronger—think about those dolls and guns.

Flash forward four years and boys and girls are even more different, with girls better equipped for building relationships and interpreting emotions and boys gifted with a better understanding of spatial relationships—knowledge greatly in demand in complex societies.

Think "vroom, vroom." In one study, researchers found boys using words only 60 percent of the time and a variety of colorful noises the remainder, while girls use words almost exclusively.

Flash forward to elementary school. At recess, girls hang out in groups of two or three, in intimate discussion. They're making eye contact, connecting, building relationship. As often as not it's relationships they're discussing—with parents, teachers, siblings, other friends. They choose games like hopscotch and jump rope, where everyone gets a turn. Differences in skill are minimized and the atmosphere is supportive.

Girls want to be liked.

Boys, on the other hand, freshly sprung from enforced immobility, are raucous, rowdy, rambunctious. They play in large groups in a constant struggle for one-upmanship that serves to reveal the leader—top dog, alpha male—of the pack. Their games are structured and complex and focused on scores.

Boys want to win.

This presents a problem, as nowadays many educators regard the normal play of boys with disapproval. In the early 1970s, Gloria Steinem said, "We need to raise boys like we raise girls"—thus blessing "girl" behavior as the norm and boy behavior as aberrant. American educators picked up this theme and ran with it, restructuring our education system for girls and disrupting boys' natural patterns of activity, attitudes, and behavior.

Competition is out in the classroom. Games with winners—

even musical chairs—have been usurped by cooperative activities. If that sounds good to you, it's because you're a woman! Studies consistently show boys do better in competitive environments.

Today's elementary classrooms are more geared to the success of girls. Coming into kindergarten, boys are more immature: besides their need for more gross motor activity, they learn to read later and their fine motor skills (finger grasp for writing) are usually behind. One way to compensate is to have boys start school a year later—an option many parents choose.

"Choice" should be the operative word, but increasingly for boys it's not, as the culture insists on regarding girl behavior as normal and boy behavior as aberrant. When Hasbro Toys tested a new "unisex" playhouse, they found the girls dressed and kissed and played with the dolls, while the boys catapulted the toy baby carriage from the roof. Hasbro's conclusion: boys and girls are different.

Some experts, on the other hand, read such boy behavior as indicating a propensity to violence. Gloria Allred, a feminist attorney, said, "This is just an argument why we need to socialize boys at an earlier age, perhaps, to be playing with dolls."

This line of thinking shows a lack of respect for the unique qualities God has built into boys—the qualities that will someday make them men worthy of the label. For example, the famous not wanting to stop for directions comes from the same sense of "I can do it" that enables my husband to figure out how to get to and fix a plumbing leak without relying on someone else. The tunnel vision that keeps the men in my life from noticing things that need to be picked up will eventually make them capable of the intense focus needed to build a business or career.

We women are different. We've got a lot going on in our minds at any one time. And our radar's always running. We're relational. We see the world from a different perspective.

I must confess, I used to think these qualities made women

superior. When Tripp and I married, I was bossy and dominant. With my own strong leadership tendencies, I would never have trusted him to lead. It took many years as a believer for me to realize that my own leadership needed to be channeled appropriately, that I needed to give up my need to control and allow my husband to lead. It was scary at first, but before long I was able to relax and enjoy the wonderful feeling of having our marriage work in a way that was pleasing to God.

Don't get me wrong. I don't think women should be doormats, either. But just as doormats need to learn lessons in not being walked on, bossies need to give up control. Both could learn a lot from really studying the story of Esther—how she had to grow as a woman, developing the courage to speak up when she should but also having consideration for the subtleties that would enable the king to hear what she had to say.

At first, as a feminist-newly-turned-Christian, I hated that story. It seemed like such an oppressive situation that Esther couldn't just barge in and blurt out what she needed to say. But that's because I was a barger and blurter. I didn't really respect my husband and his own needs.

Eventually I realized that my ability to see warning signs or to think how things impact others doesn't make me superior to Tripp—they are simply qualities God built into me so I would be better able to help my husband and children. He has his vision, he leads; I see where he might stumble and I warn—thus he becomes a better leader.

That's important.

As I gave up control, I also found ways to communicate to Tripp his tendency to deflect my input—some of which was very important. Word pictures helped a lot. They say men are more visual than we are, so if I felt he was not willing to listen, I'd remind him of King Xerxes holding out the gold scepter to signal to Esther that he was ready to hear what she had to say.

If we disagreed about something not such a big deal, I learned to let it go. After all, Tripp should be free to make mistakes. But if I feel something is important and he's squashing the discussion, I sing a few bars of James Taylor's "I'm a Steamroller, Baby" and he gets the point.

I've had to admit and apologize to Tripp for the years I didn't have the understanding of or respect for men that a man needs in a wife. That understanding and respect was built largely because God gave me the responsibility of raising eight sons. Through years of up close and personal observation, I can say I really think God knew what He was doing when He made them the way they are. And I completely understand that things that tend to drive women crazy are only the flip side of the incredible potential God gives them to be leaders and visionaries and strong husbands and fathers.

Remember how I learned to observe other mothers? Well, I've never really stopped, and one thing I started seeing after my sons were born was how we women had a tendency to squash the boyness out of our boys. It's a direct outcome of that feminist thought that has tried to characterize boy behavior as aberrant—but I see many otherwise wise mothers make that mistake.

Boys have to grow up free to be boys in order to become men. And we do want them to become men, because the ever-increasing dominance of women is really not a pretty sight at all.

Raising boys directly challenged my desire to control. With eight of them, I've had to do a lot of letting go. I didn't want my oldest son to play football because he might get hurt. But I let him and he got hurt and he was more of a man for it. And while everything in me wants to yell, "Stop!" "Watch out!" "Be careful!" I've bitten my tongue as my sons roughhouse and wrestle. I've learned to respect that they are who they are and they need to express it without constant interference from women.

What does this have to do with being "just a mommy"? Simply this: A woman has to be secure in her femininity—in the gifts God has given her as a woman. But she also needs to understand and respect masculinity. This mothering thing is a highly specialized endeavor.

Over the years I've found it takes a lot of concentration and focus to learn what it takes to be good at my mothering craft. And I'm not talking about learning to cook and clean and sew—although those are useful pursuits that boys and girls alike need to know.

When God said, "It is not good for the man to be alone. I will make a helper suitable for him" (Gen. 2:18), He did not mean someone who would cook and clean for him but someone with specialized powers of perception and information-gathering who would be able to fill in the blanks for him. Likewise, He didn't invent motherhood so kids would have someone to cook and clean for them but someone who would be their first and best teacher.

I've always found it fascinating that throughout the animal kingdom, the young progress so quickly. A foal walks within minutes after birth. Our children take at least nine months to walk independently. What was God intending when He extended the term of dependency so long for us, the very ones created in His image?

He wanted relationship. He wanted the kind of intimacy and trust that come from knowing each other through and through. And knowing our children through and through takes a lot of time.

For years, there's been a lot of talk about quality time vs. quantity time, as though you can separate and schedule them. But quality time isn't something you can schedule. Sure, you can work all week and decide to go to the zoo with your children on Saturday. But that doesn't make the zoo visit quality time.

Quality time happens on the child's terms, not yours. You can't force it or predict when it will happen—it just bubbles up when it's ready.

Quality time happens when a mother is just there doing her own thing—folding clothes, cooking dinner, typing at the computer—and her child comes in to share something or ask a question or discuss a problem. It happens when you pick up your fifth grade daughter at school and she needs your help figuring out why someone is mad at her. It happens when you're doing the dishes together and your high school freshman confides about a friend who wants to show him a pornographic web site. It happens when your children want to show you their projects, sing their songs, rehearse their lines, describe their homeruns.

When you're "just a mommy," you have more time to watch and wait and pray. It takes a lot of observation of your children to know who they truly are, and it takes a lot of thought and prayer —which is more easily done in a laundry room than in a board room—to hear the still small voice speak to you about each one.

God didn't invent motherhood so kids would have someone to cook and clean for them but someone who would be their first and best teacher.

I know the measure of confidence my children have in me, their comfort level in keeping no secrets, and their respect for my opinions is a direct result of the fact that I've always been there for them.

Does that mean it's easy? Heavens, no! It doesn't mean that I do it perfectly or that I never blow it with a hasty comment or brush-off.

It often takes a lot of discipline to choose to focus on what children say. I have to remind myself that what may not seem so important to me can be a very big deal to them. I have to remind myself when they want to talk to stop and make eye contact and really put something of myself into it.

Why do I do it? Because Jesus said, "Whoever welcomes one of these little children in my name welcomes me; and whoever welcomes me does not welcome me but the one who sent me" (Mark 9:37). I'd say that makes it pretty clear.

I'm not putting down working mothers. But working mothers are now enjoying respect and affirmation from society. They don't need someone to champion their cause. Women who opt to be stay-at-home mommies do. One outspoken woman is Dr. Laura Schlessinger, who thinks women should choose between motherhood and career. Like her, I've got to wonder why a woman would choose to have children and then leave them 30 to 60 hours per week with another woman. Add in 60 to 70 hours for the kids' sleeping and whatever travel time is, and there's not much time left to be Mommy.

That doesn't mean I don't occasionally entertain thoughts of how nice it would be to act and dress and talk like a grown-up every day.

But then I'd be missing the opportunity to live out the mandate, "He must become greater; I must become less" (John 3:30). I'd no longer be jolted by reminders—impossible messes, embarrassing situations, and humbling moments—that it's not about me at all.

This is why I speak of motherhood as not a job, but a calling —perhaps more akin to missionary work in terms of the opportunity it gives us to become more like Christ each day. It's something we do for our children, but it's also something we do for Him—giving up worldly pursuits that bring more wealth, status, and respect. It means going for long periods of time without the stimulation of adult conversation. It means always feeling frumpy next to well-dressed working women—the degree of frumpiness being directly related to the number of children you're "just a mommy" for. It means learning to live on a daily basis with no outer affirmation—no paycheck, no special awards, no applause, only the knowledge that what you're doing is something very special, very pleasing to the Lord.

Remember? He said so: "Whoever welcomes one of these little children . . ."

Just imagine how pleased He must be if you've welcomed two or three or four or five! Then thank Him for making you "just a mommy."

8

A Little Extra

My son Jonathan has a little extra. A little extra enthusiasm, a little extra innocence, a little extra charm. Oh, and did I mention an extra chromosome? The one on the 21st pair that inspires so much fear in so many parents-to-be. Named for the doctor who first described the syndrome in 1866—John Langdon Down— now referred to by geneticists as Trisomy 21. Like I said, third chromosome, 21st pair.

I suppose at one time I was fearful about Down syndrome, at least in a vague sort of way. With babies arriving every 18 months in our family, it was a topic that came up with great regularity in my obstetrician's office. By the time I'd had four or five children, we had a familiar routine. I could count on him at each first pre-natal visit to bring out the chart showing my Down syndrome odds increasing and recommending tests. And he could count on me to refuse.

This in spite of the fact that the odds had risen steadily since I had Jasmine and Samantha in my 20s (1 in 1,000), Joshua at 34 (1 in 400), to my pregnancy with Jonny at 44 (1 in 35). "What difference would it make?" I'd say to my doctor. "We want whatever baby God sends us."

But an unspoken footnote rattled: "And besides, God wouldn't send us a baby with Down syndrome because He knows with seven kids already that would be more than I could handle."

Yeah, right. Those were the days before I'd learned that God actually does sometimes give you more than you can handle— just so you'll have to ask Him to help you.

The pregnancy proceeded pretty much the same as all the

others—actually better than my last pregnancy with Sophia when I spent the last two months in bed for high blood pressure. As usual, I was beyond impatient toward the end, and the kids and I were putting together endless jigsaw puzzles, which brought out the obsessive in me and was the only thing that could make me forget I was waiting for a baby.

The birth announcements were addressed and stamped, just waiting for the specifics to be filled in. I'd established a reputation for getting mine out faster than anyone else—a source of pride, I must confess. On the front of the cards, I'd carefully penned a verse from Elizabeth Barrett Browning, "God's gifts put man's best dreams to shame." Tripp and I had sometimes taken some flak for the size of our family. After our fifth child, his mother refused to acknowledge my pregnancies, though she enjoyed her grandchildren thoroughly once they were born. We liked to remind our family and friends that children are gifts, and for Sophia had used this scripture: "Every good and perfect gift is from above, coming down from the Father" (James 1:17).

Not that it feels like a good and perfect gift when you're toughing out your eighth birth with no anesthesia. Sadly, because I got on the natural birth track with Samantha back in the days when they didn't have good alternatives, I didn't discover epidurals till I gave birth to Madeleine, a year after Jonny was born. How I wish I'd thought outside the box about that area of my life!

As usual I yelled at everyone, "I can't do this!" and grabbed Tripp's arm to tell him I had to get up and go home, but it was too late. Jonny was born.

"It's another boy!" Tripp said excitedly, and then followed the nurse as she took the baby briefly to the warmer to suction him, then wrapped him in a blue blanket and gave him to me.

"He looks a little different," I said, musing over his features with Tripp. "Look at his eyes, and his ears are so tiny."

All of a sudden, my doctor and nurse dropped the usual

postpartum routine, coming up on either side of the bed, each putting a hand on my shoulders.

"I have some hard news for you," my doctor said.

"He has Down syndrome, doesn't he?" I said. My doctor nodded, very sad.

"Well, I always said that would be all right," I reminded him. I smiled.

"We always said we wanted children in our house forever," Tripp said. "We'll name him Jonathan." It was a new name, one we hadn't talked about.

You could have heard a pin drop. And then I realized it had been quiet from the time Jonny was born, and that they would have probably waited to give me the dreaded news, but my comments had forced the situation. And who could explain the incredible feeling of joy and exhilaration I felt that God had blessed us with a child with Down syndrome—as though we were poised at the top of a roller coaster and in for the ride of our lives.

"God must love me very much," I thought.

My situation was different from others, I know. After all, we already had seven "normal" children. But there were other things God had used to open my heart and prepare the way for Jonny.

There was Amy, a six-year-old cutie pie from church we babysat for now and then to give her mom a chance to get out by herself. Amy's dad had left shortly after her birth—just couldn't get into having a daughter with Down syndrome.

On the brighter side was the dad and daughter duo I'd seen a month before riding the merry-go-round at a nearby amusement park. Now I think God orchestrated the picture for me. I couldn't take my eyes off the two of them—a gleeful almond-eyed three-year-old, a father helplessly in love. *There's something special here,* I thought.

And there has been.

Experts told us we would need to work a little extra to help

Jonathan realize his potential. What they didn't know was how God would use Jonathan to help us realize our own.

I remember us all lying on our stomachs around him, cheering mightily as he lifted his wobbly head a few inches from the floor. Down syndrome children have low muscle tone, making it more difficult for them to meet each physical milestone. So we taught Jonny how to sit, how to crawl, how to feed himself—the things other children learn without much help at all.

We were thrilled as Jonny mastered each new goal. And I was thrilled at the unexpected blessings following his birth. My children were growing more caring and compassionate every day. A stronger unity was being built in our family.

So we all understood when one day Matt said, "Wouldn't the world be a better place if everyone had a brother with Down syndrome?"

Maybe it would.

Jonathan was followed a year later by our daughter Madeleine, who's "normal," if you consider a little girl who could belt out tunes like Ethel Merman to be normal. We call her "the voice heard 'round the world."

Because of Jonny's delays, they grew up like twins, learning to babble, play, and walk together. Even today, at 10 and 11, they are still that close. When I am out with Jonny, he always wants to buy something for Madeleine. And when I'm out with Madeleine, she always wants to bring something home for Jonny.

As Jonny and Maddy were toddling around together, Tripp and I decided that with all we'd learned about raising a child with Down syndrome, it would be a good thing to use that expertise to raise another, plus it would mean a special bond between two brothers.

Adoption is another thing that's easier said than done. We went through the home study process, explaining things like why with nine kids we'd want another, especially another with Down syndrome, to social workers who weren't so familiar with the word "calling." And we were just about complete when we found out about a baby boy who'd just been born in southern California the day before. Unfortunately, because his surprised and overwhelmed parents had signed him over to the state within hours of his birth, he was already in the foster care system. But after two months of winding our way through the bureaucratic red tape— think DMV only a hundred times worse—we were finally able to bring Jesse (which means "God exists") home.

That was the end of our plan but evidently not the end of God's. A couple whose prenatal test showed their second child would have Down syndrome sought us out for advice because the mother wanted to get an abortion and the father didn't. We invited them over to share the upside of Downs, only to have them ask us to adopt their baby when he was born. We agreed to go through the rest of the pregnancy with them—doctor's appointments and all—and prepare to receive the baby if they didn't change their minds. They didn't. So we ended up bringing Daniel home from the hospital two weeks before Jesse's first birthday.

Looking back, I wonder how in the world we managed. We had a lot of help from Jasmine, whose Prince Charming had not yet arrived. I was pretty organized and had a little help with housecleaning. But mostly we managed, I believe, because we were obedient.

So many times, people say, "Oh, I could never do what you do," "It takes a special person," or, most sadly, "I wanted to have/ adopt more children, but my husband/wife didn't want to." First of all, anyone could do what I do. It doesn't take a special person —you already know I was probably the girl least likely to succeed at motherhood.

The only thing going for me is this: I learned to listen for the still small voice. I learned to trust it over conventional wisdom and the advice of others. And I learned to say yes. I also was blessed with a husband who was willing to trust God and take risks.

It involves risk-taking to be obedient. God says, "Adopt another baby with Down syndrome," and Tripp and I say yes. We're not thinking what it will be like 10 or 12 or 20 years down the road. We're just thinking, "Oh, adopt a baby? That's doable." It's been eight years since we adopted Jesse, and he turned out to have some other issues that made raising him more difficult than raising Jonny had been. There was a time when I felt I'd hit a wall, that God had asked too much of me.

But He hadn't. And I got over it. And I'm glad I obeyed.

Another moment I almost faltered—three years ago when an agency called to ask if we'd consider adopting another baby with Down syndrome.

"No!" I exclaimed automatically. "I'm 52 and I'm getting tired. I just don't think I have it in me."

A few of my kids overheard me saying no, and when I got off the phone, they argued, "But, Mom, you always said you wanted 12!"

"Oh please say yes, Mom," Sophia pleaded. "Then we can be *Dirtier by the Dozen!*"—her unintended combination of the book about a family with 12 kids and the war movie her brothers had watched a few weeks before.

That was the beginning of our adoption of Justin, a Taiwanese boy born in the States to young parents attending college here on temporary student visas. I later learned that we were at the bottom of the agency's list—because of the number of children we already had. But Justin's parents had just not clicked with any of the prospective families they'd been sent to meet.

They clicked with us and immediately liked the idea of their son growing up in a big family with other brothers with Down syndrome. They also explained they were giving him up because they wanted him to be raised in an American family. In Taiwan he would be placed in an institution and would not receive the education he would here. He'd never reach his full potential. And he would be mistreated and misunderstood.

Thank You, God, that I live in this country. I can think of no other place in the world where disabled citizens are treated with such care and concern. The number of people on Jonny's professional school team—the special teacher and assistant, speech therapist, physical therapist, occupational therapist, and all the time we put into meeting to discuss his education and his progress reminds me of 1 Cor. 12:22-23: "On the contrary, those parts of the body that seem to be weaker are indispensable, and the parts we think are less honorable we treat with special honor."

So it is a special honor to have them in our family. Matt. 26:40 promises, "I tell you the truth, whatever you did for the least of these brothers of mine, you did for me."

But we haven't gone the extra mile to earn God's favor or a place in heaven. Jesus already did that work for us. It's just that having been lifted out of a life of darkness and into the light, I'm so dazzled by God's glory and generosity that I want to give back a little extra myself. When I give back, when I am obedient, I feel His pleasure.

I want to be like the sinful woman (Luke 7:37), whose love for Jesus led her to a sacrificial act so vivid it was recorded in all four Gospels. Though three Gospels don't give her name, some people assume she is Mary Magdalene. John 11:2 clearly identifies her as Mary, sister of Martha.

Mark 14:3-9 tells the story of how she brought an alabaster jar filled with perfume to anoint Jesus. She broke the jar and poured the perfume over His head. Luke says she was weeping and that her tears fell on Jesus' feet, that she wiped them with her hair and kissed them and poured perfume on them.

Mark records that some who witnessed this event rebuked the woman sharply—especially because the perfume was worth a year's wages. It could have been sold to raise money for the poor. Imagine! A year's wages at the feet of Jesus.

What would it be like to see Him face-to-face, to weep over His feet, to wipe them with my hair and to anoint them with perfume? As a woman who lived a sinful life, I can only imagine how satisfying it would be to completely forget myself and others, to break my own alabaster jar and release the precious contents inside.

Saying yes to God's call to add more children to our family through adoption was the closest I could come.

But the surprise has been how I feel as though God broke an alabaster jar and released its precious contents on me. For surely these four boys have transformed me. Yes, parenting them has been more of a challenge. But with the adversities has come an expansion of my heart. The tenderness I feel for them has generalized to the wider population. I am a better person because they are in my life.

And so are all the other people who come to know them.

Jonny has always been fully included in a regular classroom in school, with a special teacher who modifies the curriculum for him. Each spring his team—teachers, specialists, parents—meets with the teacher whose class he'll be going into. Usually the teacher looks worried—how do you accommodate a kid who's years behind his classmates academically, whose speech is sometimes impossible to understand, whose greatest triumph in third grade was learning to use scissors adequately? I usually give a little pep talk about the beauty of full inclusion, then I let it be.

School starts in September. By October the teacher is completely in love with Jonny. In fact, I can count on the end of each school year receiving a letter from Jonny's teacher telling me what a wonderful experience it's been to have him in the class. I've never received such a letter from my other kids' teachers.

Jonny's public school kindergarten teacher, after 30 plus years of teaching, said she'd never seen children as loving and caring as Jonny's classmates. The secret, she said, was Jonny. When he graduated from her class, she wrote us: "As the Bible says, 'The Lord does not look at the things man looks at. Man looks at the outward appearance, but the Lord looks at the heart.' Jonny certainly taught the children and me to look at the heart; for he has a very big heart!"

She confirmed what I'd seen all along whenever we meet new people. Jonny has a way of breaking the ice before others can think too long about their response to a child who is—well, just a little different. Then he brings out the best in them. Remember when cynics presented a blind man to Jesus and asked who had sinned, the man or his parents, that the man had been born blind? Jesus answered that neither had sinned, "but this happened so that the work of God might be displayed in his life" (John 9:3).

I suppose most have understood this to mean that the work of God would be displayed when Jesus healed the man's blindness. I see it differently. After all, Jesus didn't say the work of God would be displayed in his healing. He said it was displayed "in his life."

That blind man was once a baby and a growing boy. For years his needs had an impact on his family, his friends, his teachers, his community. Surely the work of God was being revealed each day in the growing compassion and wisdom in those who might otherwise have had no reason to give up their own self-centeredness.

Remember the birth announcements I'd prepared before Jonny's birth? *God's gifts put man's best dreams to shame.* We sent them out with a note about his extra chromosome and our great love for him. Later, we found Jonathan's name means "gift of God."

And he has been a gift—a gift I never would have thought to ask for, bringing lessons I never knew I needed to learn. The greatest surprise is this: Our life together has been less about my helping him reach his potential than about him helping me reach mine.

Sometimes when we're in a museum or a mall, in the middle of a good laugh, I catch someone off-guard, looking uncomfortable and standoffish. I know that as long as we live some will see Jonny as having a little less. I've learned he has a little extra. And so does our world because he's here.

≈≈≈≈≈≈

What will be your little extra? It might not be a baby with Down syndrome, but surely as you continue your spiritual journey, God will drop something in your lap or whisper something in your heart that will give you the opportunity to grow and change, to enlarge your capacity to love, to teach you compassion, and to depend on Him and love Him more.

I remember a couple whose life was perfect. When I first met Gary, he was a youth pastor, filled with charisma. He met a beautiful young woman and they had a romantic courtship, engagement, wedding—with a cloud of awestruck teenage witnesses. When they had their first baby, they brought her to all the teen gatherings, where she received enough attention to last any little girl a lifetime.

Jasmine was a teenager then, with five younger siblings under eight. We were surprised when Gary and Anne called to invite our family over for dinner.

"The whole family?" I asked.

"Absolutely," Anne said.

I couldn't remember the last time someone had invited us to dinner. I mean, it's just too formidable an undertaking to invite a family of eight over. What's more, I knew Gary and Anne and Hannah lived in a teensy two bedroom apartment.

I tried to let her off the hook, but Anne was determined. Even though it rained that day and the kids wouldn't be able to play outside, she insisted we come over.

We arrived to find the living room stripped of furniture and a big blanket on the floor. A big yellow sun hung from the ceiling and little black ants crawled along the wall—all handmade by Anne and Hannah. Their kitchen table, covered with a red check tablecloth, was crowded with hot dogs, hamburgers, and all the fixin's.

What a blessing to have someone prepare something so appealing to our kids. And what a blessing to set aside time to get to know each other better.

A year later, Gary and Anne had another baby. So did we. When Jonny was in the hospital for the third or fourth time, Gary came to visit and to talk. He'd obviously been doing a lot of thinking.

"You know, so far our life's been too easy," he said. "I know somewhere along the way we're going to have to deal with something hard. It scares me, but I know it's coming. Otherwise God won't be able to accomplish much with us."

A short time later, Gary accepted a position as youth pastor at a bigger church. We heard the news of a miscarriage, and then another. As anyone who's had one knows, miscarriages are more devastating than most people realize. I've had a few myself and know they can hit you as hard as losing a full-term baby. In some ways it's worse because so few understand how much loss a mother feels.

But because of what Gary had said to me, I knew he and Anne would be the better for having gone through their particular "little extra."

You may have already gone through a little extra—and maybe a few times. But if you haven't, don't be afraid. Or if you're afraid, try like Gary to hold onto the idea that no matter what happens, God will use it to help you grow.

Sometimes it's something you didn't choose, it just happens —like the birth of a baby with a disability, or the loss of a child. I once met a mother of 12 who'd lost her two oldest sons when they picked up a downed electrical wire. How hard that had been for her, I can only imagine.

Sometimes it's something you're supposed to choose, as when God nudges parents to adopt a baby, or even to have more themselves. I know several families who already had four, five, or six children when the husband opted for a vasectomy. Years later, when the still small voice began to speak to them, they listened. Then they saved their money, traveled to a good specialist in the Midwest, and had the vasectomy reversed. All of them have had babies since—some more than one! And I'm guessing they can't imagine life without those "little extras."

The point is, we have to be ready for the little extra in our lives and not be afraid. We must be ready to embrace it, no matter what form it takes. God may ask you to do things that are almost impossible to explain to others. I know our vasectomy-reversed friends took enormous flak from friends and family, including other believers. But their faith in God and His direction for their lives gave them the courage to see it through.

Another family we knew with an insurance salesman dad, mom, and four kids was rocked when God called the parents to be missionaries in India, necessitating that the two youngest teens be sent away to school. At the time, I have to admit, I questioned whether God would really call someone to the mission field. Now, with all I've learned of the mysteries of how God works in people's lives, I'd never presume to judge.

If you feel God nudging you and you feel yourself balking, give it time. Remember how Samantha knew God wanted her to homeschool before she became willing? Remember how I first turned down our third adoption? I remember, too, my friend Liz, homeschooling mother of seven with plenty to keep her busy. One Sunday she confided that she felt God wanted her to take responsibility for the children's ministry at church. "I can't believe it, but I'm actually starting to want to do it," she said.

Are you ready to accept the "little extras" that God may send your way?

It's a little like the yeast we put in bread dough. It takes awhile to rise. Likewise, God plants an idea in your heart and then nurtures it—as long as you don't bury it or push it aside. When I think how we might have missed the opportunity to have Justin —sweet little Justin with his consistently cheerful and loving presence—in our lives, I thank God that I was willing for another "little extra."

Just the other night, our family watched an old favorite of ours, *Parenthood,* which never fails to make me laugh until I cry. Definitely not a Christian worldview movie (warning: if you watch with kids, have the fast-forward button handy for just a few scenes), but I love it because it's filled with compassion for all the imperfect but mostly well-intentioned parents it portrays. That's the way I think God must be full of compassion when He sees our mistakes.

The most down-to-earth parents are Gil (Steve Martin) and Karen (Mary Steenburgen), who already have their worries with an anxiety-ridden 10-year-old—their own "little extra." Karen confides to her sister-in-law that she loves being "just a mommy," that she feels she's good at it, and she'd love to have another baby. But when she finds out she's pregnant, her husband has just lost his job. He's upset and she accuses him of wanting her to have an abortion. He says it's her choice, when what she wants to hear is his commitment to the baby.

In the midst of his tantrum, his live-in grandmother comes in with this story:

Grandma: You know, when I was nineteen, Grandpa took me on a roller coaster.

Gil: Oh?

Grandma: Up, down, up, down. Oh, *what a ride!*

Gil: What a great story . . . (sarcastically)

Grandma: I always wanted to go again. You know, it was just so interesting to me that a ride could make me feel so frightened, so sick, so excited, so scared, so safe, and so thrilled, all together! Some didn't like it. They wanted to go on the merry-go-round. That just goes around. Nothing. I like the roller coaster. You get more out of it.

(Grandma leaves to wait for them in the car as they're on their way to see their two oldest kids in the school play. Gil looks after her like, "Hunh?" and makes a sarcastic comment.)

Karen: I happen to *like* the roller coaster, OK? As far as I'm concerned, your grandmother is brilliant.

Gil: Yeah, if she's so brilliant why is she sitting in our *neighbor's car?!*

At the play, their youngest child, a handful and a half, gets upset and rushes onstage, causing complete pandemonium. Some people are laughing, but some are angry because the show is ruined. Gil—who worries a lot about what people think—is completely distraught, looking almost nauseous. Suddenly, we hear the unmistakable roar of the roller coaster and Gil and Karen begin weaving across the screen like they're in the front seat with all the people in cars behind. Gil's terrified, but when he sees how much Karen is enjoying it, he starts to relax, and by the end of the ride, signaled by the whoosh of the roller coaster sliding to a stop and the crowd's emotions subsiding, he is a changed person. He puts his hand on her belly and smiles, accepting the future.

The beautiful ending to *Parenthood* is one that most people miss. Flash forward a year to see all the new babies the family has produced—including Gil and Karen's. Most people wouldn't notice—unless they knew one themselves—that they've had a little girl with Down syndrome. Good thing Karen had pledged allegiance to the roller coaster. And good thing Gil decided it might not be so bad after all.

Parenthood—motherhood—is a roller coaster. For some it's easier than others to be ready for the ride. But to enjoy it, you have to stop resisting and controlling and just go where it takes you. You have to be ready for the belly flops and heart stops. It always looks to me as though the ones having the most fun are the ones brave enough to lift their arms in surrender and just *let go*. And for believers, the beauty of letting go means we're letting God.

You can be sure of one thing: God knows what wonderful plans He has for you as a mother! And He will be there to lift you and sustain you through the incredible adventure ahead.

May you find the joy of letting go and letting God. May you accept your imperfection as God does. May you bask in His unconditional love and do your best to pass it on to those He's given to your care. May your troubles "melt like lemon drops," serving only to remind you to put your trust back in Him. May each day be new and filled with wonder. And may you and your family rest always in the peace that passes understanding.

Notes

1. **Les Miserables** is a novel that belongs on every Christian bookshelf. I was a new believer when I first saw the musical and was emphatically touched by this tale of grace and redemption. Since then, every reader in our family has read or listened to the reading of the book at least twice. There are so many themes for family discussion—despair vs. hope, condemnation vs. redemption, works vs. faith, and legalism vs. grace. We might listen to a lifetime of sermons and really never "get it" about these topics. But Hugo uses characters to make them easy to see—just as Jesus used stories to teach us too.

2. **Down syndrome** is a condition occurring in 1 out of every 800 children in which an extra chromosome is found on the 21st pair. Though limited in intelligence, children with Down syndrome—especially when raised in loving, supportive homes—can grow to be actively contributing members of society, bringing their own unique gifts to their school and work environments. As the mother of four children with Down syndrome (one by birth, three by adoption) I know emphatically that Down syndrome is not an unhappy ending, just the beginning of a different kind of story.

3. **A simple statement of faith** is all it takes to begin a relationship with God—something like, "I know I've fallen short in my life, and I know I need You. God, I accept the sacrifice Jesus made for me on the Cross, and I will count on Your Holy Spirit to guide me from this day forward." I promise you, that if you say such a prayer, you will find your life beginning to change in ways you never dreamed possible. And you will feel God's presence and love, more and more each day.

4. **Montessori** is an educational approach based on the idea that children are born with "sensitive periods" when they are most receptive to certain kinds of learning. These include concentration, independence, order—in addition to academics like reading, writing, and math. If the child is presented with appropriate cues during the sensitive period, learning will be easy and filled with joy—resulting in a child who grows up eager to learn more. If the sensitive period is missed, the child will learn with difficulty and

feel resistant to future learning. Since the sensitive periods all begin before we enroll children in kindergarten, we need to be aware of the child's needs and try to provide for him or her. The best time to begin engaging the child in household chores, for example, is when he or she shows interest—as when your two-year-old picks up a broom to sweep. We just need to make the task possible and accept the child's less-than-perfect results.

Using Montessori methods at home to help your child grow to be the best learner he or she can be is the topic of my first book, *Small Beginnings: First Steps to Prepare Your Child for Lifelong Learning.*

5. **Homeschooling** is a special calling. Those who heed it deserve our highest respect, as they are literally laying down their lives for their children each day. I know because I homeschooled my children for a full seven years, then smaller numbers off and on through the years as we made different plans each year based on each child's individual needs—as well as the family's. Currently, all our children attend public school, but Tripp and I are still vigilant about overseeing their education. My own experience has taught me never to judge a parent's educational choices, as we can assume that God nudges each parent toward what He wants for their children.

6. **Overpopulation** is a popular myth, but a myth nonetheless. The United States birthrate is currently less than replacement level, and if it weren't for immigration, our population would be declining. This is true for many industrialized nations. The myth of overpopulation can be easily refuted by doing the math, as did Mary Pride in her book *The Way Home.* She calculated that if we gave each person in the world 2,000 square feet of living space (the size of a small home), we would all fit into the state of Texas.

Proponents of population control use the threat of overpopulation to justify abortion. They also blame overpopulation for famine and starvation, overlooking the real problems of tyrannical governments and mismanagement of resources. For the facts, do a Google search (www.google.com) for the words "overpopulation" and "myth" for many thought-provoking articles and statistics.

7. **The Four Spiritual Laws** are a simple explanation of our need for Jesus and how we can receive Him. They were written nearly 40 years ago by Bill Bright, the late founder of Campus Crusade for Christ—and have since introduced countless thousands to a true relationship with Jesus Christ. They are the last words Tripp and I heard before becoming believers.

You may view the Four Spiritual Laws with applicable Bible verses and a diagram for each one at http://www.crusade.org/fourlaws. Stripped to their essence, they are: (1) God loves you and has a wonderful plan for your life. (2) Man is sinful and separated from God. Therefore, he cannot know and experience God's love and plan for his life. (3) Jesus Christ is God's only provision for man's sin. Through Him you can know and experience God's love and plan for your life. (4) We must individually receive Jesus Christ as Savior and Lord; then we can know and experience God's love and plan for our lives.

8. **God and family planning** don't often wind up on the same page. For Tripp and me, they did after the birth of our fourth child, Matthew, in 1987, when we made a decision to trust God with the size of our family. Although we didn't know God in a personal way then, but only as an impersonal source of power, we felt led to make this covenant, "We will stop using birth control and accept as many children as You want us to have; and we will trust You to provide for them." At the time, we were thinking in terms of material provision, but interestingly, in less than a year, we came to know God in a personal way, thus our children were provided for spiritually by having parents who could raise them with a strong and loving foundation.

We have met many other parents who have taken the same step, realizing that if we can trust God with every other area of our lives, we can certainly trust Him with this one too. We ended up with 12 children—9 by birth, 3 by adoption. If you're inclined to trust the Lord with this area of your life, but worry you might have 12 too, just remember, God has a different plan for each family.

A life-changing book for many is *A Full Quiver* by Rick and Jan Hess, available at my web site www.barbaracurtis.com.

9. **Giving to the poor** was a question that troubled me for many years. Living near San Francisco, we encountered countless souls with cardboard signs and hands out. For a long time, I tried to discern which were worthy recipients, wondering, "Will this one just go out and buy booze?" or judging, "This one looks sincere." Then I decided it should actually be simpler than that. As a believer I should just follow God's instructions: "Whatever you did for one of the least of these brothers of mine, you did for me." Then it's between God and the recipient what happens next.

10. **MOPS,** as Mothers of Preschoolers is affectionately known, began

with eight women meeting in February 1973 in Wheatland, Colorado, and has now grown to an international organization offering support and resources to mothers in all walks of life—stay-at-home moms, working moms, teen moms, single moms, and so forth. There are over 2,700 MOPS groups meeting across the United States and in 19 other countries. You can find a group near you at http://www.gospelcom.net/mops.

11. **Birth order** is a big part of what makes us the way we are. For instance, a higher percentage of political leaders and CEOs are oldest or only children. Some researchers say oldest children actually have more in common with each other than with other members of their own families. It's helpful to understand your children in terms of their family placement. For more information from a Christian perspective, see Kevin Leman's book *The New Birth Order Book: Why You Are the Way You Are.*

12. **Toy guns** were strictly forbidden in the Curtis home in the early 1980s. What would you expect from a former antiwar radical feminist still under the illusion that girls were normal and boys were not? No violence for our family—for years I'd even avoided killing the occasional household spider.

However, I had no control over the fact that my four sons were so gun-obsessed that they found every scraggly branch or sausage link capable of rapid fire. At toy stores, after loading up with things nonviolent, I'd have to drag them drooling from the artillery aisle. What if my repressive rule were to backfire, compelling them to become all I'd tried so desperately to keep them from becoming?

So it was strictly strategic when I lifted my toy gun ban. Only later, after a few more years of observation and developing a more teachable attitude, did I have enough confidence in my own femininity to not find symptoms of masculinity threatening. Mothers, let your boys be boys!

13. **Early feminists** were definitely down on abortion. Susan B. Anthony, now featured on our currency, wasn't thinking of political correctness when she referred to abortion as "child murder." Nor when she wrote, "No matter what the motive, love of ease or a desire to save from suffering the unborn innocent, the woman is awfully guilty who commits the deed. It will burden her conscience in life, it will burden her soul in death; but oh, thrice guilty is he who drove her to the desperation which impelled her to the crime!"

Elizabeth Cady Stanton, with her antislavery perspective, wrote, "When we consider that women are treated as property, it is degrading to women that we should treat our children as property to be disposed of as we see fit."

Mattie Brinkerhoff weighed in thus: "When a man steals to satisfy hunger, we may safely conclude that there is something wrong in society—so when a woman destroys the life of her unborn child, it is an evidence that either by education or circumstances she has been greatly wronged."

14. **Antifeminist backlash** among the younger generation is evidenced in a steady stream of books with titles like *What Our Mothers Didn't Tell Us: Why Happiness Eludes the Modern Woman* by Danielle Crittenden, *Domestic Tranquility: A Brief Against Feminism* by Carolyn Graglia, *Who Stole Feminism?: How Women Have Betrayed Women* and *The War Against Boys: How Misguided Feminism Is Harming Our Young Men* both by Christina Hoff Sommers. These are not books written and published by Christians, either.

This is a hopeful trend, for it signals more support for women who exercise their option to choose—to choose to make motherhood a priority.

Barbara Curtis is available for speaking engagements on a wide variety of topics for women of all ages. She also teaches writing workshops.

You may contact Barbara at megamommy12@aol.com or through her web site: www.barbaracurtis.com

or write her in care of:
Beacon Hill Press of Kansas City
P.O. Box 419527
Kansas City, MO 64141